First Indian on the Moon

First Indian on the Moon

Sherman Alexie

Hanging Loose Press
Brooklyn, New York

Published by Hanging Loose Press, 231 Wyckoff Street, Brooklyn, New York 11217. All rights reserved. No part of this book may be reproduced in any form without the publisher's written permission, except for brief excerpts in critical articles.

Printed in the United States of America
10 9

Hanging Loose Press thanks the Literature Program of the New York State Council on the Arts for grants in support of the publication of this book. The author thanks the National Endowment for the Arts for a Creative Writing Fellowship.

Acknowledgments: Some of these poems first appeared in the following publications: *Beloit Poetry Journal, Caliban, Hanging Loose, I Would Steal Horses* (Slipstream Publications Chapbook), *Left Bank, New York Quarterly, Red Brick Review, Red Dirt, The World, and ZYZZYVA*.

Cover art by Eric Gansworth. Photo by Denise Wood.
Cover design by Caroline Drabik.

Library of Congress Cataloging-in-Publication Data

Alexie, Sherman
    First Indian on the moon / Sherman Alexie.
        p.   cm.
    ISBN 1-88241-303-2 : — ISBN 1-88241-302-4 (pbk.) :
    1. Indians of North America—Literary collections. I. Title.
PS3551.L35774F5   1993
818'.5409—dc20   93-29630
                                                          CIP

CONTENTS

All I Wanted To Do Was Dance

Influences

*where i have been
most of my lives is
where i'm going*
—LUCILLE CLIFTON

**for Kim and Arlene
and Lillian**

Influences

We waited in the car
outside the bar
my sisters and I
"for just a couple drinks"
as we had heard it
so many times before
as Ramona said
like all Indian kids
have heard
before

from their parents, disappeared into the smoke and laughter of a
reservation tavern, emerging every half-hour with Pepsi, potato
chips, and more promises. And, like all Indians have learned, we
never did trust those promises. We knew to believe something
when it happened, learned to trust the source of a river and never
its mouth. But this is not about sadness. This is about the stories

imagined
beneath the sleeping bags
between starts
to warm up the car
because my parents trusted me
with the keys.
This is about the stories
I told my sisters

to fill those long hours, waiting outside the bar, waiting for my
mother, my father to knock on the window, asking *Are you warm
enough? Are you doing all right? We'll be out soon, okay?*
Sometimes, we refused to open the locked doors for our parents,
left them to gesture wildly and make all of us laugh because there
was nothing else left to do. But this is not about sadness. This is
about the stories

I created
how I built
landscapes and imaginary saviors.
Once, I dreamed a redheaded woman,
gave her name and weight
and told my sisters
she would rescue us
from our own love

for this mother and father who staggered from the bar always five minutes before closing, so they could tell us later *At least we left before last call.* But we did love them, held tightly to their alcoholic necks and arms as we drove back home, stole the six-pack they bought *for the road* and threw it out the window, counted mile markers and coyotes standing on the edge of the road. But this is not about sadness. This is about the stories, those rough drafts

that thundered the walls
of the HUD house
as my sisters and I lay awake
after we finally arrived home
and listened
to my mother and father dream
breathe deep
in their sleep, snore
like what you might want me to call drums
but in the reservation dark
it meant we were all alive
and that was enough.

Year of the Indian

January

New Year's Eve, out with my girlfriend and ten other friends, everybody white except me. We were all in the pizza place in Reardan, just off the reservation, when the door opened and this Indian stranger walked in, just blasted, and sat at the counter. He gave me a nod and smiled, one Indian to another.

Then my girlfriend leaned into the middle of the table and we all leaned into the middle of the table to hear what she had to say.

"I hate Indians," she said.

*

Oh, my first brief love.

February

Temperature below freezing, but the entire population of the Spokane Indian Reservation watched as Lester FallsApart stumbled out of his tin shack this morning and checked the length of his shadow.

That shadow stretched for miles down the tribal highway, ran past pine tree and Coyote Springs, right down to the very edge of the reservation where it stopped, grew darker.

Spring may never come.

March

So many Indians in the Breakaway Bar on St. Patrick's Day, drinking green beer and talking stories.

"What you giving up for Lent this year?" Seymour asks me.

"Catholicism," I tell him.

And we laugh.

"Hey," he asks. "Did you ever hear about the guy who was half-Irish and half-Indian?"

"No," I say.

"He owned his own bar but went out of business because he was his own best customer."

And we laugh.

And I buy him another beer and then another. One, because he's Indian all the time, and two, because he's Irish today.

We've all got so many reasons, real and imagined, to drink.

April

How would your heart change if I told you Jesus Christ had already come back for the second time and got crucified again?

He called himself Crazy Horse and never said anything about a third attempt.

May

Today, Moses wanted to memorialize every Indian who died in war, fighting for this country and against this country during the last five hundred years, so he began the task of capturing swallows, one for each of the dead.

Moses held each swallow to his mouth and breathed out the name of a fallen Indian: man, woman, child. But those names are secret and cannot be shared with you.

Moses worked for years. After he was finished, Moses released the swallows into the air over the reservation, millions of them.

Millions.

*

Fly, warriors, fly.

June

June begins and ends with a powwow and there are powwows everywhere in between.

That is how it should always be.

*

Arlene, my sister, she says, "Before this month is over, the best traditional dancer in the world is going to call me sweetheart."

*

June begins and ends with a powwow and there are powwows everywhere in between.

That is how it will always be.

July

Fourth of July and the air is heavy with smoke and whiskey. I find Tyrone passed out in the dumpster behind the Trading Post. I reach in, slap his face a little, tug on his arms and legs.

"Hey, cuz," I say. "Wake up. Someone's going to come along and throw you away."

He doesn't move. Tyrone was my best friend in the reservation grade school. In sixth grade, he was so perfect and I was nearly as good. Once, Tyrone and I took on the rest of our class in a basketball game. Two-on-thirteen, full court, regulation time, and we beat them by twenty points. But that was a century ago. Now, Tyrone is too far gone to swat at the flies that crawl into his open mouth.

"Hey, Tyrone," I say. "Come on. Somebody's grandma is going to think you're salvageable and take you home with her."

He doesn't move at all. He is breathing, though, and I jump into the dumpster with him. I try to lift him but he's too heavy with alcohol and commodity food. I can't get any leverage.

"Hey," I yell at the Trading Post manager as he walks by. "Help me get Tyrone out of this damn thing. The garbage men might not see him in here."

"Don't worry about it," the manager says. "They stopped collecting that kind of trash a long time ago."

Listen: all I want is a little piece of independence.

August

Sweet songs from the tribal drum and the mosquitoes, both driving me crazy in my bed when I try to sleep.

These end of summer days drag on with no measure other than Indian sweat and hot tempers. Ernie Game punched Seymour thirty-seven times the other night because it was 7:37 p.m.

This kind of heat creates that sort of twisted logic.

Ten years ago, Little Dog drowned when he passed out and fell face down into a mud puddle, probably the only mud puddle left in that year of drought. It was so strange that the tribe created a holiday for it. No one worked and no one drank in celebration. We all just sat around and laughed at the stupid wonder of it all.

And last night, after everyone had gone on home, I stood naked on my front porch and howled like an old coyote and the old coyotes, beautiful and crazy, howled right back.

September

Working at the Laundromat seven days a week. Change for dollar bills, sweeping up stray detergent, amusing little white kids.

All for minimum wage.

It's Labor Day and I'm supposed to honor the sweat that made my sweat possible. My hands are bleached white from drop-off laundry; my feet and back ache because I'm always at attention, never use the employee's chair that sits in the back office. I'm always doing an awkward fancydance between washer and dryer.

All for minimum wage.

I punch a clock when I make promises now; I punch a clock when I tell lies. Every day I feel dirty and used. I'm a dishrag, cloth diaper, mismatched sock.

Come on in, sir, I have beautiful braids. Come on in, madam, I have granite cheekbones, and my clothes, my work clothes, my blue shirt and blue jeans, are clean, clean.

October

In the shopping mall today, a little white boy ran up to me, shouting so loud that he attracted everybody's attention.

"Hey, mister," he yelled at me. "You're an Indian and I'm dress-

13

ing up like an Indian for Halloween, too!"

There were smiles and laughter all around. I smiled and laughed a little, leaned down and whispered into the little boy's ear. His smile quickly disappeared and he ran toward his mother, crying.

The crowd circled me, accused me of child abuse, demanded apologies and explanations. But I just left before mall security could arrive to question me and before some group of rednecks could gather enough courage to jump one crazy Indian.

*

"Son," I whispered into that little boy's ear, "I'm just wearing my nice Indian mask today. If I take it off, you'll see the warrior that wants to cut your tongue out."

November

Walking down the tribal highway, hungry, wondering where my family will find their food during the long winter, when a truck rolls by me, stops.

"Hey, chief," the driver asks. "Where the hell am I and how do I get out of here?"

I tell him he's on the Spokane Indian Reservation and that I'm not really sure how to get out.

"Ha, ha," he laughs. "That's a good one, chief. Now, really, how do I get out of here?"

I point down the road and tell him he just needs to follow the road he's on, stay on the pavement, don't make any turns until you cross water, then it's a left to the rest of the world.

"Thanks, chief," he yells.

As he drives away, a bag drops off the back of his truck and I run over, pick it up, and nearly cry because it's a fifty-pound bag of potatoes. Then, I do cry because it's potatoes, potatoes, potatoes.

*

We give thanks, Lord, for the food we're about to receive.

December

Crazy Horse dresses up like Santa Claus for the reservation school Christmas Pageant, reads the letters of all the Indian boys and girls asking for jobs, college educations, a ticket for a Greyhound travelling back or ahead five hundred years.

Crazy Horse searches his pack but he only finds a few hard candies, an orange, and miles and miles of treaties.

Crazy Horse leaves out the back, straight into the Breakaway Bar, where he watches a holiday movie, Bing Crosby singing *White Christmas* for choirboys who go home afterward and open their presents, all finding rifles, hammers and nails to build walls.

14

Scalp Dance by Spokane Indians

*Before leaving Spokane Falls, Paul Kane dropped down to
the nearby village of Kettle Falls to paint his now-famous
"Scalp Dance by Spokane Indians" in oils on canvas. Its
central figure, a woman who had lost her husband to the
Blackfeet, whirled around a fire swashing and kicking in
revenge a Blackfoot scalp on a stick. Behind her, eight
painted women danced and chanted, as did the rest of the
tribe to the beat of drums.*

—from **The Spokane Indians: Children of the Sun** by
Robert H. Ruby and John A. Brown

Always trying to steal a little bit of soul, you know? Whether it
be poetry or oils on canvas. They call themselves artists but they
are really archaeologists.

Really, that's all any kind of art is.

And who am I, you ask? I'm the woman in the painting. I'm the
one dancing with the Blackfoot scalp on a stick. But I must tell you
the truth. I never had a husband. The artist, Paul Kane, painted me
from memory. He saw me at Fort Spokane, even touched his hand
to my face as if I were some caged and tame animal in a zoo.

"I need to memorize that curve," he said.

In fact, I have never shared tipi and blanket with any man.
When Paul Kane touched me I struck him down and only the hur-
ried negotiations of a passing missionary saved me from Kane's
anger. But far from that, I am also a healer, a woman who reserves
her touch for larger things.

Paul Kane was nothing except an artist.

But you must remember Kane was also an observant man. He
watched many Spokanes put themselves to death. He thought it
was because of gambling losses. But no, it was because of all the
loss that the Spokane Indians were forced to endure.

Like the loss of soul I felt when I found myself in that painting
years later. Ever since Paul Kane had touched me that day, I had
felt something missing: a tooth, a fingernail, a layer of skin.

You must also understand that we treated Paul Kane well even
as he conspired to steal. Some sat still for his portraits and didn't
smile because Kane insisted they remain stoic. That was his great-
est mistake. Our smiles were everything; our laughter created por-
traits in the air, more colorful and exact than any in Kane's work.

I have seen all his paintings and Kane never let us smile. When
you see me now in that painting, dancing with the scalp, you
must realize that I didn't have a husband, that I never danced
without a smile, that I never sat still for Kane.

That is the truth. All of it.

Reservation Drive-In

The French Connection

"Drive, damn it, drive," Seymour yells as we fishtail through the reservation drive-in at noon, weave between speaker stands, over speed bumps, circle the snack bar where pioneers cower and refuse to let go of their popcorn. Once again, we chase the tail of some Crazy Horse dream, chase the theft of our lives. What matter if there's a case of beer bottles in the back seat? What matter if Seymour is farsighted in one eye and nearsighted in the other? What matter if the drive-in manager calls the Tribal Police? What matter if the change in the ashtray is only enough gas money to get us halfway? What matter if we break into the projection booth and run the movie in broad daylight? What matter if Gene Hackman drives us quickly into the unsteady future?

Rocky

Do you remember those Yakima Indian boys played the theme song from *Rocky* ninety times straight one summer day in 1978, played it on secondhand trumpets, played it in their garage, door open wide, the first and last reservation amphitheater? They were always barefoot, their toes so Yakima we all knew they didn't belong on the Spokane Indian Reservation, but there they were: the barefoot, bareback, Yakima Indian boys' secondhand trumpet duet. Do you remember the name of that goddamn song? Was it *Gonna Fly Now,* and did they fly after their station wagon, packed full of reservation souvenirs, left all of us Spokane Indians behind? Didn't Arnold find one of those trumpets years later in the trash and blow it hard, blow air loud until he couldn't breathe, his heart punching against his rib cage?

Enter the Dragon

Suddenly, the Indian boy is Bruce Lee. Maybe he's only the Bruce Lee of the reservation playground, kicking every other child aside on his climb to the top of the slide. *But tell me, Mr. Lee, what's the use?* There is no soundtrack for the rest of that Indian boy's life, no sudden change in music to warn him of impending dangers. Mr. Lee, in your last movie, in your climactic battle with Han in his hall of mirrors, it was beautiful when you smashed those mirrors and won the war with yourself, that interior battle. But you died soon after that movie, Mr. Lee, and never finished the next. Now, there is a photograph of the Indian boy kneeling beside your Seattle gravestone. He looks straight into the camera; he does not know what comes next.

Star Wars

Dick from Somerville calls in the middle of the night. "The next astronaut to set foot on the moon is to be an Indian," he tells me. I walk out into the reservation starry night where the moon hangs low on the horizon, another bright and shining promise, another measure of the distance between touching and becoming. Sometimes, it is too much to ask for: survival. There are too many dangers, a fresh set of villains waiting for us in the next half-hour, and then in the next, and the next. They murder us, too, these heroes we find in the reservation drive-in. The boy, Luke Skywalker, rises up against his dark father and the Indian boys cheer, rise up and fall out of car windows, honk horns, flash head-lights, all half-anger until the movie ends and leaves us with the white noise of an empty screen. Over and over, we make these movies our own promises, imagine our fathers never lose, pretend our mothers slice their skin a hundred times in testament. Soon, we will sit around old drums and sing songs: "You promised us the earth and all we got was the moon."

The Bicycle Thief

Charlie Chaplin was a Spokane Indian. He was drunk in the Breakaway Bar when someone stole his bicycle. For weeks, he waddled around the reservation on foot, his Levi's hung low on his hips, nothing surprising—until another bicycle was stolen from between the phone booths outside Irene's Grocery, and then a bike was missing from the community center, then two from the Longhouse. The Tribal Police Chief had no comment, the Tribal Council called a general meeting but not one Skin arrived. Every Indian was on foot. They walked and walked, raised arms in greeting, but never said a word. The bicycles were all gone but not one Indian said a word. Charlie Chaplin was braiding his hair when he cleared his throat and said, "Now." Surprised by the sound, he said it again, louder, shouted it as he ran across the reservation. "Now," he said. He said, "This is not a silent movie. Our voices will save our lives."

A Reservation Table of the Elements

Air is between these words,
fanning the flame.
—LINDA HOGAN

for Mary

Genetics

Fire
follows my family
each spark
each flame
a soldier
in the U.S. Cavalry.
First

it was the fire in 1973. Flames dropped from the attic of our old
house and burned every quilt we owned. Cousins and neighbors
came from miles away to carry furniture, clothes, our smallest pos-
sessions from the house, but they all arrived too late to save
much. All we had left

was a family portrait
singed
curled at the edges
all of our dark skin
darkened
by ash and smoke damage.
Next

was the trailer fire in Montana that stole my oldest sister, stole her
husband, stole her little library of books that included a few she
had borrowed from me. All I could think, all I could ask when I
found out about the fire was *Did my books burn?* Since then,
we've lost three cars to electrical fires—1981 Chevy Blazer, 1978
Ford Mustang, 1984 Ford van—the last while my younger sister
was driving it along Little Falls Dam and she looked

into the rearview mirror
and saw flames rising up.
She was listening
to Freddy Fender
when it happened, listening to
Before the Next Teardrop Falls
when she stopped the van
turned off the radio
jumped out and ran down the road.
She made it a few feet
when the van exploded

and knocked her over. When the Tribal Cop heard on his radio
that a car was burning down at Little Falls Dam, his first thought

was *Those damn Alexies and their goddamn cars.* He told my sister that, as they both watched the van burn down to bare frame. The Tribal Cop told my entire family that, when he drove my sister back to our house. We all laughed at the odds, not because they were astronomical, even though they were. We laughed at the magic of it all

> laughed
> at how precise
> every little pain can be
> laughed
> at the fire
> that threatened us
> continually
> laughed
> when the Tribal Cop
> asked my father
> if he smoked

and my father said, "Only when I'm on fire." Some nights, I have this dream that my family sits down to dinner. I want it to be Thanksgiving dinner but I cannot be sure. We sit down to dinner and one by one, we all spontaneously combust, until we are just piles of ash on secondhand chairs. Then, my grandmother

> Big Mom
> comes back
> to sweep us up
> with her traditional broom
> sweeps us all
> into her beaded bag
> and carries what
> remains
> into the next life
> into the next element
> and I don't care
> if it's earth, water, or wind.
> I just want
> to be done
> with fire
> with flame and ash.

Fire Storm

1.

The highways are closed
between Spokane, the city
and Spokane, my reservation.

Fires everywhere; smoke; zero visibility.

The local news interrupts the national news
to tell me I won't be going home tonight.

Five hundred years
and nothing has changed.

2.

On January 13, 1981, my sister Mary and her husband Steve died
in a trailer fire. After a long night of drinking, a curtain drifted on
wind from an open window, touched the hot plate left burning,
and created this ash I gather now. My sister and her husband too
drunk to hear the smoke alarm, passed out in the back bedroom
while the flames grew up and drew swords. *Yes.* I create cruel
images for flames, give them names like Custer or Columbus. I
give fire simple life and hate so I can assign exaggerated love and
invent acts of heroism. He died trying to pull Mary from the
house; her wild pony hair survived the heat.

3.

Crown: to provide with something like a crown.

The fire
crowned
the trees
above my head.

The fire crowned
the trees
above my head.

The fire crowned
the trees above
my head.

The fire crowned
the trees above my head.

The fire crowned the trees
above my head.

The fire crowned the trees above
my head.

The fire crowned the trees above my head.

4.

Often, in this poetry, we steal words, gather kindling, twist
newspaper, circle rocks, and wait for the flame. We create
metaphors to compensate for what we have lost.

The fire did not crown above my head. The fire crowned above
the head of a local news reporter who stopped tape and escaped.
I watched the news and they replayed the event: as flames
climbed up pine trees just behind him, the reporter detailed the
stupid courage of homeowners with garden hoses. The camera-
man was already backing up, his disconnected voice shouting "We
gotta get out of here! We gotta get out of here!"

Here, I imagine the reporter saw the flames reflected in the
eyes of his cameraman, in the eye of the camera. Here, I imagine I
saw the flames reflected in the eyes of the reporter. Here, I imag-
ine I touched the television screen and heat blistered my fingers.

The fire crowned the trees above my head.

5.

**FIRES CONTINUE TO BURN OUT OF CONTROL TONIGHT IN
EASTERN WASHINGTON AND NORTHERN IDAHO. EQUIPMENT
HAS BEEN GATHERED AT PAINTED HILLS. FIREFIGHTERS SAY
THEY WILL MAKE A STAND AGAINST THE FIRE THERE.**

Here, I make my stand. I refuse
fear and anger exploding like flame.

My heart a burning barrel.
My hands dark as obsidian.

Here, I make my stand. I refuse
pain and grief quick like lightning.

My eyes matches striking.
My skin singed newspaper.

Here, I make my stand. I refuse
loneliness and inertia crawling like napalm.

My rib cage a barn fire.
my hair a crown of flame.

6.

SPECTACULAR BARN FIRE SEEN FOR MILES

A fire fueled by exploding barrels of oil and gasoline destroyed a barn in Moran Prairie Saturday night, creating a spectacular display onlookers likened to an Independence Day show.

The barn, a chicken coop and an old car
were transformed
to mounds of charred rubble. Shades

of blue and yellow brightened
the night sky
as the fire reached

inside. "I could see the fire
from my living room."
Above the horizon, the barn

like a workshop contained
oil, paint, paint thinner
and other highly flammable substances.

Firefighters do not yet know what started the fire, but believe it may have been accidentally caused by someone who had been using a cutting torch inside the barn earlier that day. The cause of the blaze is still under investigation.

from *The Spokesman-Review*, October 13, 1991

7.

In this vision, Mary gives birth to flame, a child that flames with its first breath of oxygen and explodes with its first taste of failure.

In this vision, Mary wears a crown of fire; this royalty frightens me into silence.

In this vision, Mary pours her heart across hot rocks in the sweatlodge and the steam that rises is called love.

In this vision, Mary fancydances through smoke and ash, holds her open hand over candle flame and kisses my forehead.

In this vision, Mary is medicine: she is forgiveness and penicillin; she is survival and aspirin; she is courage and cough syrup.

In this vision, Mary is magic: she is a card trick and my protector; she is a mirror and my future; she is a rabbit from the hat and my song.

8.

No one will believe this story, so it must be true.
—Lester FallsApart

The phone call a cigarette in the dark, my *Hello* shaped like a question mark.

"Junior, don't go to school today. Your dad's coming to get you."

"Why?"

"I don't want to talk about it over the phone. Just get ready. Your dad will be there pretty soon."

I dressed, brushed my teeth, combed my hair into braids. No, I dressed, brushed my teeth, but my hair was too short for braids.

"Junior, what're you doing?" Betty asked. She was the white woman who owned the house where I boarded during the school year.

"Mom called earlier. She said my dad's coming to get me."

"Why?"

"I don't know."

She was in bed with her lover, Don, a thirty-five year old bus-boy at Denny's. Once, he slapped me hard across the face after I listened to his first edition album of *Sergeant Pepper's Lonely Hearts Club Band* without his permission. No, he punched me hard in the stomach after I scratched his copy of the Stones' *Exile on Main Street.*

The 60s still break hearts.

Betty and Don were in bed when my father arrived, his hair and heart unbraided. He stood in the kitchen next to the coffee maker; I stood by the refrigerator. The house was so cold our breath was visible. No, the house was so cold frost formed on the walls. Betty and Don refused to leave the bed.

"What is it?" I asked my father.

"Mary and Steve died last night."

Arrows to the heart.

"How?"

"House fire."

I walked into the bedroom where Betty and Don waited for warmth. The house was fueled by oil and it took an hour or two before anyone could feel heat from the morning furnace. No, the house had one fireplace in the living room that needed a fire built every morning.

Every morning, I lay awake and waited for someone to build that fire. Robert Hayden wrote a poem about that blueback cold of a fireless morning, how his cold father rose to cut firewood and twist newspaper, break kindling and build that austere love.

The morning my sister died there was no fire built.

"Betty," I said. "I have to go home. My sister died."

"Oh."

"Can you call the school and let them know?"

"Sure."

I turned to leave the room and my father was standing in the doorway. He was a large man grown small with age and alcoholism. He possessed neither questions nor answers.

"Goodbye, Betty," I said.

"Wait. Do you think you can build us a fire before you leave?"

The cause of the blaze is still under investigation.

9.

fire sale: a sale of merchandise damaged in a fire.

Here, I offer what I own, change
my references and gather ash

from the roads I've traveled. Heart
lost in a couch fire; heart fallen

to ash after the slight touch
of fear. Here, I offer what I own:

old guitar, pair of shoes, basketball
on fire. I've got asbestos hands

and bare feet walking over hot coals.
I've got three flames tattooed

under my left eye, barn fire
in the living room and a burning barrel

on the television. Here, I offer
what I own and what I don't own

is the difference between touching
and becoming. My enemies, real and imagined,

are torches, matches, cigarette lighters.
My enemies love me; my lovers burn oxygen

like flame. Here, I offer what I own:
this crown of flame, this skin scarred

and blistered, this sinner curled
like blackened leaves

in the hands of an angry god.
Here, I offer what I own: grief

like a burning bush that shouts
forgiveness and never forgives.

Family Cookbook

Fry Bread

I am the cook at every wake, buried up to my elbows, laying out flat the bread, the plates. I've seen them all die, the old of cancer, screaming out the names of Indians been dead for a hundred years. The young, dead in car wrecks, pieced back together by the undertaker and laid out like a quilt in the coffin. Yes, I've held every Skin by the hand on their long walks past survival. And I have seen the Indian boys with their braids cut off, hoping to look presentable, like God was a crew cut football coach making the final cut, like being Indian was a varsity sport. I wonder what happens to their braids. Maybe the undertaker keeps them pinned to a wall in his basement, maybe he gets drunk and shows his friends. I hear them laughing, laughing.

Pepsi-Cola

Fifty cents, fifty cents, all our dreams coming true for two quarters, five dimes, ten nickels, who cares about the pennies. We are beautiful in our braids and Levis outside the Trading Post. *C'mon, I promise I'll buy Pepsi this time.* Yes, we've got those dumpster dreams, those sweet and sour smelling dreams, dreams that used to be good and edible, the dreams that rot, changed into the dreams of flies and wasps. *I'm a legal eagle. Hey, Georgie, I'm legal, enit?* Listen up: you got wings, I just want a couple feathers. You got a car, I want the stuff falls between the seats. You got an orange, I want the rind. You got a dollar, I want *E PLURIBUS UNUM.*

School Lunch

Ain't got free milk today. Not today, no way. You goddamned Skins got to buy your milk today. No, I want fruit punch, I want a tall glass of water, throw it down your blouse. I eat my macaroni & cheese with an Indian fork, season it with Indian salt and pepper. *Do you remember Robert Harris?* Yes, the reservation white boy, so poor he got free milk even when the milk wasn't free. Shit, the cows felt so sorry for him, they'd give him the milk personally. *Hey, hey, Frenchy, there's a fight at lunchtime. Who's fighting? Junior and Paul Corral.* Indian versus Indian. All the Indian boys and girls surround them in a circle and fancydance until they wet their pants. You Skins been drinking too much milk, goddamn it. Ain't got free milk today. Not today, no way.

3 a.m. Chili

Early, early, early, before the powwow has seen its third sunrise, me and Lester FallsApart are eating chili with too much commodity cheese. Seymour comes along and tells us the chili will give us nightmares, make us think we're white CPAs. "No way," says Lester, "not if I don't sleep." So, we're awake for 88 hours straight, no need for whiskey; our visions come to us in surround sound. Mine is Darth Vader and he keeps telling me *I'm your father, Victor, I'm your father.* Lester's telling me he sees a dozen Indians riding bareback on kangaroos, chasing the Seventh Cavalry who are riding gophers. We tell Seymour what we saw and he says "So much for history."

Black Coffee

What does it matter if it's hot or cold? It was sitting in the blue pot on the black stove in the green house. Big Mom's house. Everybody drinking it, cup after cup, except me. I wanted its magic, its medicine. I picked up the blue pot with my bare hand and it burned, *burned.* Big Mom pulled me away, dragged me outside and forced my hand into the snow. I remember the steam rising. I remember the smell of my own flesh burning. It does matter if it's hot or cold.

Old Salmon

Sisters, do you remember the old salmon we found, the salmon so old we thought eating it would give us wisdom? There was too much we didn't know about survival. After the second big bite we knew we were wrong. The salmon had made promises it couldn't keep. The salmon was not in love with us; we should have never loved the salmon. Sisters, on the long ride to the hospital, did you see the same sky outside the car window? I saw stars, dizzy, indistinct, falling. You both have the same eyes and hair, the same half of the same memories, twins. Did you see the same thing as I did, did you see the same thing as each other? I remember my hand in my pocket because I thought there was something to lose.

Occupational Hazards

Working graveyard shift at a 7-11
in Seattle, making minimum
everything, when I got robbed

by a guy with a pistol. Now
I was thinking as it happened
thinking the gun ain't loaded

everything is under control
this guy don't want to hurt me
he understands I ain't got much

more than he does. I got
an old car, high rent, even
the same dark skin as his

and my best shirt is the one
I have to wear to work
with 7-11 stitched on my chest.

But the robber takes me back
into the cooler, makes me
kneel on the cold floor

with my hands on my head/ my back turned to him/ and I wet
my pants when he puts the pistol/ up against my skull/ I keep
thinking/ I'm going to die/ between the broken eggs/ and the
expired milk/ and I keep thinking/ I'll make a move/ on the
robber/ and tear the gun from him/ and I keep thinking/ I'd
rather die fighting/ and/ I'd rather die brave and crazy/

but the robber laughs, runs
out of the store, out
of the rest of my life

and leaves me to the police
and their sketch artist.
It takes hours to describe

the robber, detail by detail
the color of his hair, eyes, skin
his height, weight, age

all approximated, estimated.
After all that work
the sketch artist asks

if I've remembered everything
perfectly, if I'm sure
I've described the robber

exactly as he looked, exactly
as he lived and breathed
and I tell the sketch artist

"Yes, I could never forget"
and then he shows me his sketch
shows me my memory, my vision

and the face on the page
is the same face I always see
when I look in my mirror

in those last seconds
before I walk out the door
and leave home for work.

A Twelve-Step Treatment Program

Communicate

Been on the wagon for a week, I tell the whole bar and the Waitress brings me glass after glass of water.

Eight cups of water a day is what a person should drink to ensure proper health, I read on the wall in the IHS Clinic, but what does the USDA recommend for the alcoholic Indian dreaming the Seventh Cavalry storming his mirror?

Sometimes after all the snakes and breaks and shakes are gone and you don't wake up sweating beer and you think you'll never touch another shot of whiskey again, you walk into the Breakaway Bar, see another skin drinking and you want it all back again, too.

Educate

Summer heat breaking my mirrors so I dig up a handful of quarters and go to a two-dollar movie for the air conditioning, find myself a good seat and an old friend, another Indian college student, holding tight to a big check, some student loan or another. We end up together at the bar on a nothing going weekday and talk stories all night long until he says his advisors at the college he attends want to save him from a semester of incompletes. He only has a couple weeks to finish them all, to pick up his degree and the dream he has of Icarus.

"Listen," he tells me, leaning over the table between us, his mouth an inch from the edge of his glass, his braids dragging on the floor. "My advisors sent me this letter advising me to discard my cultural baggage and concentrate on the future. I wrote back advising them that maybe all of us Indians don't drink so much because we're Indian. Maybe we drink so much because all of you are so white."

Instill Self-Esteem

I go to the Indian Center looking for a job, so they send me out to a senior citizens' home that needs a janitor. So I spend nights mopping floors until last week when some Indian woman I never seen or heard before about two minutes from dead all the damn time wakes up while I'm emptying her waste basket.

She looks at me and says, "I knew your grandmother."

That makes me laugh but then she says, "She was always so tall."

My grandmother was six foot easy, so I drop my broom and run out, until I get here where I'm good and safe, hiding behind a locked door and my failed dreams, where I can be a dime store Indian instead of the real kind.

Give Love and Time

I walk by the Trading Post where Lester FallsApart is drinking alone.

"I got secrets," he tells me.

I pretend I don't hear him.

"Hey," he says. "I got secrets but ain't nobody wants to hear them."

Then I walk over to Lester, sit down on the curb beside him. He offers me his bottle of wine and I take a drink without even bothering to wipe it clean.

"Cousin," Lester calls me.

"Brother," I say.

Teach Values

"Why are Indians such good Catholics?" the Bartender asks the Professor from out of nowhere and the Professor, she takes a drink, clears her throat and says, "Because they're so willing to forgive their own sins."

The Bartender sets an empty glass in front of me but it's so clean that I begin to forgive him. "Why do you drink so much?" he asks me and I tell him it's because I'm 75 percent Indian and about 90 proof Catholic.

There's more than one way to survive.

Talk About Drugs

"I have this aunt who's blind," Junior tells me. "She's scary because she knows who you are even if you don't talk to her. I walked up to her once and before I said anything, she said 'Hello, Junior.' Sometimes, I wonder if she's really blind."

"Maybe it's some Indian medicine," I tell Junior, just kidding, but he nods his head in agreement.

"How did she go blind?" someone asks and Junior says, "She and a bunch of her friends drank antifreeze, thinking it was a jar of bootleg and everyone died, except my aunt, because of that shit."

The Professor at the end of the bar asks, "Did you know you inhibit the effects of antifreeze on the body by pumping that person full of ethanol?"

Junior looks at me, looks at the Professor, and asks, "Really?"

"Yes," the Professor says, "And all for want of a drink."

Discipline

I am in the Breakaway Bar drinking with a few of my friends when my dad walks in with a few of his friends.

"Ya-hey," my father yells. "I'm going to buy my son a drink."

"Ya-hey," I yell. "I'm going to buy my father a drink."

Just then, my grandfather walks in, sits down between my father and me and whispers, "Hey, I'm a little short on cash. How about you two buy me a few drinks?"

Establish Rules

A sign posted above the mirror behind the bar: WE DO NOT ACCEPT PERSONAL CHECKS OR PROMISES.

Stop the Enabling

Waiting for the checks, all of us dry, a few with the snakes, talking to people been dead for years, when the Professor walks in and she's always got money since she teaches at the community college. So we hit her up for a few beers and she laughs at us, calls us alcoholics. I tell her maybe she is, too, but she says, "I only drink beer and only on weekends."

I don't think that makes any sense, especially coming from the Professor, and I'm about to say so when Lester FallsApart runs in, waving his General Assistance Check above his head. My mailbox is a mile away, so I'm out the door, walking as fast as I can, holding my dreams an inch from my chest, making it easier to breathe.

Motivate

"Hey, listen, chief," the State Trooper says. "We don't want to take you to jail, okay? And you don't want no DWI on your record. So just climb in the back and sleep it off. I'll come back and wake you up in a few hours, okay?"

Simon climbs into the back of the van and dreams of large, beautiful Indian women.

Seek Help

Two in the morning and I've been on the wagon for a year when my older brother calls me from the tavern.

"Hey," he says. "Can you come down here and help me carry this keg home? It's too damn heavy for me to do it alone."

I hang up the phone and go back to sleep.

Help Others

Four in the morning and I've been sober for one year and two hours when my older brother calls me from the tavern.

"Hey," he says. "I've been waiting. Are you coming to help me carry this keg home or what?"

I hang up the phone, pull on my shoes and clothes, and go out to change my life.

The Alcoholic Love Poems

1.

Alcohol is a drum
calling me. Alcohol

calls me. Sometimes
it's so hard

not to hear
that drum. Sometimes

it's so hard
not to dance.

2.

You told me once that the best sex we ever had was one winter
night in February after I had spent the whole day drinking. I made
love to you drunk, during a blackout, and can't remember any of
it. After you told me, I wanted to know if I had used another
woman's name, not because I loved someone else. I wanted to
know because my imagination always increased when I was
drunk and I wouldn't be surprised to discover I had used some
movie star's name. But no, you said I whispered your name all
night, even after I passed out, whispered your name with this
mouth, sour with beer and that old lie about never drinking again.

3.

Is alcoholism genetic
or conditioned? I ask

myself as I weave
through another reservation

maze of treaty
and unrequited love, find

a bottle of vodka
and a box of commodity cheese

at the end, call myself
an ordinary victor, another

victim of science
and its necessary research.

4.

My hands shake sometimes
because I love you
and other times
because my body remembers
detoxification
so I ask you not to drink
beer, whiskey, vodka
before you come to see me. Please

brush your teeth, wash your hands
if you must have even a little
because I was never as strong
as I wanted. The taste of alcohol
even in the slightest of kisses
will make me forget who I have become.

5.

The difference between need and want must be explained. I quit
drinking 450 days ago. I quit drinking 450 days before I quit you.
Then, driving downtown today, I saw that same old Indian wino
who must have borrowed a thousand quarters from me over the
years. It was the fifteenth consecutive day of sub-zero tempera-
tures and the old Indian wino was wearing a stocking cap with
the price tag still attached. He bought that damn cap instead of
booze and I bet you that cap cost exactly the same as a bottle of
Thunderbird wine.

6.

Just moments after meeting
you, I needed
to say "You're exactly
the kind of Indian I would love
to get drunk with."
But I've been sober

for two years now. All I said
was "When I used to drink
you're exactly
the kind of Indian I loved
to get drunk with."

Oh, all my life
in the past tense.

A Reservation Table of the Elements

Aluminum

1.

My father quit drinking by use of a simple formula. He bought beer only with the money he saved from recycling the aluminum Coors Light cans he emptied by drinking. At 19¢ a pound for recycled cans, it was the Reservation Law of Diminishing Returns. Nobody can be alcoholic and ecological at the same time.

2.

Little Johnny Wonder Horse lost his fingers on Independence Day when he dropped a lit M-80 firecracker into an empty Diet Pepsi and held the can until it exploded. He ran to his HUD house and tried to open the door for a full minute before he realized he couldn't turn the knob because his fingers were gone. When they asked him later why he'd kept hold of the can, Johnny said "Because I wanted to know how it would feel."

3.

Standing outside the Tribal Trading Post during a blizzard, there is nothing more beautiful than snow fallen onto the dark hair and braids of these Spokane Indians, nothing more beautiful than snow fallen onto the stray dogs and beer cans still on the sidewalk. If I light a fire in the dumpster, everything will change, transform, reinvent itself. If I light a fire in the dumpster, the Indians will dance, will forget the cold, will dance and forget the cold. If I light a fire in the dumpster and throw the beer cans in, they will burn until their brand names are gone and the Spokane Indians will sing all night long, will sing all night long.

4.

Just after Victor told Suzy that he would love her forever he grabbed a random can, took a drink, expected beer, but got a mouthful of ashes instead.

5.

Pick up a chair and smash it against the walls, swing it so hard that your arms ache for days afterwards, and when all you have left in your hands are splinters, that's what we call history. Pick up an aluminum can and crush it in your fingers, squeeze it until blood is drawn, and when you cannot crush the can into any other shape, that's what we call myth.

Hydrogen

Crazy Horse
never died.

Don't you know
he was the one

who climbed on top
of the Hindenburg

and lit
a match?

Neon

1.

Victor got a job working the graveyard shift at a neon sign factory, worked so many hours that one morning he looked at the sun, looked directly at the sun, and said "I'm not sure anymore what's real and what ain't."

2.

Homeless and hopeful, I walked down Monroe Street until I saw a neon sign in a window: ALL TYPES OF LOANS CONSIDERED. I stared through the glass until I got the attention of the white man inside. He raised his hands in that gesture which means *What the hell do you want?* I pointed at the sign and pointed at my chest, made an empty circle with both hands, and pointed at my heart. He looked at me for a while, smiled, touched his chest, and raised his index finger, meaning he only had one heart. I nodded my head and walked down Monroe Street until I saw another neon sign in a window: BUY SELL TRADE.

3.

Sometimes, it's almost nearly beautiful and almost always close to tragic when the lights of a city are reflected in the eyes of an Indian miles away from his/her reservation.

4.

If you put your ear really close to a buzzing beer sign hanging in the window of the Powwow Tavern, you can hear horses thundering, you can hear rifles, you can hear a cavalry sword leaving its scabbard.

5.

"Your mother and I fell in love in a cowboy bar in Spokane, two-stepping to a song I can't even remember. All I can remember is your mother's hair, so long and black I wanted to tell her it looked like the Spokane River must have before the whites ever showed up. Even now, when anybody asks me what is my favorite color, I just smile and say "Adell's Black Hair Reflecting Red Neon," and you know that ain't in nobody's Crayola box.

Copper

When the pipes froze
last winter

on the reservation
I crawled beneath

the HUD house
with a blowtorch

and discovered
America.

Oxygen

1.

On the night Lester FallsApart drank two bottles of vodka, I watched over him as he lay on his stomach on the powwow grounds. I listened to him breathe. Then, he did not breathe, he did not breathe, he did not breathe. I touched his arm and he started again, oxygen rushing into his body like salmon swimming upstream.

2.

During our first aid class, all the Indians told our white instructor that the CPR dummy named Annie wasn't real enough for a reservation. So we got out the crayons and gave her warpaint. "Well, if she's a warrior, what happened to her?" asked the instructor. "She had a heart attack," I said, "trying to save the rest of us."

3.

An Indian man drowned here on my reservation when he passed out and fell face down into a mud puddle. There is no other way to say this.

4.

When I was very young, I liked to stand just outside the dance hall where traditional and fancydancers would take breaks, their breath coming quick and heavy, their bodies slick with sweat and dreams. I loved their smell, the way they moved as different animals. I remember one young dancer, a Flathead boy, who was the most beautiful dancer I had ever seen. He never got tired. But I also remember that same Flathead boy running from the powwow police after the dancing was over. We ran together and hid in the rodeo grounds. He pulled out his cigarettes, offered one to the gods like a good Indian, and shared another with me. It was the first and last cigarette I ever smoked. I remember I couldn't breathe. Soon, the powwow police followed the smell of smoke, the flash of a struck match, and shined their flashlights on us. The Flathead boy punched me hard in the stomach and ran away into the dark. He left me so surprised and hurt that I never thought to run away myself. As I sat in the back of the Tribal Police Car, the deputies all made funny hand gestures, pointed at me, and laughed. I remember I still couldn't breathe.

5.

When the Indian woman kissed me, I breathed deep, tasted her stories, pulled her stories into my lungs, and they were good. It was all good.

Invitation

for John

When you visit, I'll sleep
on the couch while you sleep

in my bed. I'll leave
my best blanket

for you, take my nightmares
with me. In the morning

tell me how well you slept
and make coffee

while I crawl back, nearly
sleepless, into my bed

and leave you
to the silence

of your first cigarette
of the morning. Watch over me

as I sleep, please
shake me awake

if I begin to struggle
against the next loup garou

Shifting its shape, against
the new werewolf

too cruel to notice
its moon has gone down.

Reservation Mathematics

Mixed-up and mixed-blood
I sometimes hate
the white in me
when I see their cruelty
and I sometimes hate
the Indian in me
when I see their weakness

because I understand the cruelty and weakness in me. I belong to
both tribes. It's my personal Wounded Knee, my own Little Big
Horn. On the telephone, my friend from New York told me I
drifted back into a reservation accent only when I talked about
pain. How could I tell her

that the reservation is more
than pain?
It's double happiness, too
when I watch the fancydancers
or
the basketball players
or
the comic book collectors
all dreaming

of a life larger than this one, constructed by walls everywhere. It
doesn't matter if it's a square, rectangle, or triangle, they all mean
the same thing. They're all the direct opposite of a circle. It
doesn't matter if it's a triangle, rectangle, or square. They're all the
direct opposite of a circle. I've been dreaming of a life

with a new shape, somewhere
in the in-between
between tipi and HUD house
between magic and loss.
I'm always dreaming
of a life between
the 3/16 that names me white
and the 13/16
that names me Indian.
That's what has happened to us.
Indians have learned

to love by measuring cup. I can count up all my cousins. I can
count every can of commodities in the cupboard. I can count

every piece of broken glass on my reservation and I still wouldn't have enough of anything, neither answers nor love. But I can stand up in front of you and recite formulas; my voice will tremble and my hands will shake. I can stand up, like Lucille said, through your destruction. I can stand up, like Lucille said, through my destruction. I can stand up, like Lucille said, through our destruction, through

> every little war, every
> little hurricane.
> I'll take my Indian thumb
> and my white fingers
> on my strong right hand
> and I'll take my white thumb
> and my Indian fingers
> on my clumsy left hand
> and I'll make fists,
> furious.

House(fires)

1.

House: two doors, front and back, but James jumps out his bedroom window into the reservation snow. Last winter, I staggered against my fear as I stood on the roof and broke ice, shoveled it off onto the ground below, a small defense against the kind of collapse we saw on the 11 o'clock news.

2.

During the 11 o'clock news, Spike asked me, "Have you ever noticed how a camera turns an innocent moment into an exhibition?" I told him this reservation has no innocent moments. For instance, the photograph of our HUD house is framed and centered on the wall as evidence, but the photograph is less dependable than memory. I remember I stood at the window and watched my mother/father/sister/brother take the picture. Still, in the photograph we have now, the window where I stood is vacant, but I was there.

3.

I was there with all the drunken Indians in our HUD house just as Lester FallsApart announced his plan to jump off the roof into the teardrop of a broken hearted Indian girl as it trembled on the sidewalk, trembling there since 1966. "All of this at exactly midnight," Lester said. Seymour then told us he would reveal the location of the very last elephant graveyard, but I already knew it was behind a billboard in Spokane, still secret because the elephants disguise their bones as bottles. "All of this at exactly midnight," Seymour said. Eugene fancydanced wildly in a corner. He wanted to re-create the universe with his feet; he wanted to be the second Big Bang. The moon will forget itself and get greasy-faced on powwow chicken. The planets will eat too much fry bread with butter and grasp at their chests. An asteroid with braids will stand in one place in the bar for years. After he dies, it will be discovered his right foot was nailed to the floor. "All of this at exactly midnight," Eugene said. Suddenly, nothing happens and I'm in the backyard with the grass only our dogs will eat. Then, an explosion. Maybe the post office has changed its mind. Maybe every broken treaty has come true at the same time. Maybe Lester and Eugene have tumbled down the basketball stairs, arms wrapped around each other like reservation high school lovers. Maybe it's a new kind of drum, an enormous drum, a four-dimensional drum, a drum beating itself over the head with big sticks, a drum called *drum,* a drum called *trumpet,* a drum that sits in the bar and lies about how often it sounds like a heartbeat.

4.

"It sounds like a heartbeat," Broken Nose said more than once as he hammered nails into old wood and built his house at the exact location on the reservation furthest from anything white. When he couldn't sink a wall no matter how deep he dug into the earth, Broken Nose wept into an empty cup, but it was never enough.

5.

It was never enough, never. How do you live in a house with only three walls, the fourth wall missing and open, until every moment of your life is like the first act of a reservation high school play? Look: A fat man in braids watches television. A beautiful woman makes fry bread in the kitchen. Twin girls help boyfriends crawl into their second floor bedroom. Outside the house, an Indian boy sleeps in an infinitely blue van: Its doors are never locked.

6.

"The doors are never locked," Seymour tells me. "Stay with me on this. The doors are never locked." We walk in the front door of the house on the hill, vacated for the summer by the white teachers who have learned to leave. The refrigerator's empty but we find a jar of peanut butter in a cupboard, another small victory. Seymour tears sheets off furniture, plugs in small appliances, and runs hot water. He turns mirrors inward to face walls, replaces dresser drawers upside down, their contents ready to fall with the slightest touch.

7.

Ready to fall with the slightest touch, you crawl up a pine toward the largest tree house on the reservation. Do you remember this was the place where Steve Moses showed you the photograph of that naked Indian woman? She was the beautiful Indian who accepted Marlon Brando's Academy Award on national television and rallied against continued Native American genocide, then signed some sort of treaty with *Playboy.* Years later, you sat in this same tree house and read about that same Indian woman in *People* magazine. She said it was all a huge mistake.

8.

"It was all a huge mistake," Lester tells us. "I was drinking in Spokane and needed a place to sleep. So, I stagger on over to Dirty Joe's house, walk in and pass out on the couch. Wake up the next morning and three white kids are sitting on me, all watching cartoons on the TV. Turns out Dirty Joe got evicted and these kids belong to some couple who sleep late. I'm getting ready to leave when one of the white kids asks me, 'Are you a real Indian?' I tell him I don't know."

9.

I don't know how late it is when I deliver pizza to a burning house. "Excuse me," I say to the man who answers the door, "your house is on fire." He takes the pizza from me. "That information doesn't create in me any sense of obligation," he says and brushes ash from his shoulder. He doesn't give me a tip and I still don't know how late it is.

10.

I don't know how late it is when the Indian woman rushes from her burning trailer, throws her arms around Seymour. "Please," the woman tells Seymour, "You must save my children. You must save Jimmy, Carlos, Margaret." Seymour runs into the trailer, searches every inch on hands and knees, until nearly overcome with smoke, he crawls out, blackened by ash, defeated. "There's nobody in there," he tells the Indian woman. "I know," she says. "I'm thinking of Carlos in Gallup, Jimmy working on a fishing boat in Alaska, and Margaret standing at a thirteenth floor window of the First Interstate Bank in downtown Denver. Please, they all need to be saved."

11.

They all need to be saved during a reservation 100-degree summer. Lester is passed out for hours in the back seat of his mobile home, a four-door Chevy with all the doors closed and locked, windows rolled up tight. Years later, his hands still tremble like a divining rod.

12.

Like a divining rod, like a rabbit from a hat, like a psychic locating the body, like a flame from the fingertips of an amateur Indian magician. Something close to a burning bush, something close to pouring whiskey onto a campfire, something close to another house fire celebration.

13.

Another house fire celebration: The Indian Health Service doctor took the photograph of our house, flames leaping from the roof, but it was the house behind our own that was burning, its flames rising in another illusion. Every Indian on the reservation was there, carrying valuables from the house on fire. The firemen arrived while we were sifting through the ash.

14.

While we were sifting through the ash of a New Year's Eve house party fire, I found a shovel-shaped incisor, evidence of another unsolved crime. I keep the tooth in a pocket of my medicine jacket, a small defense against the kind of violence I saw on the 11 o'clock news. I was there when the local authorities found the body, heard the EMT say, "It sounds like a heartbeat." But that was never enough to identify the remains. On the reservation, doors are never locked and our lives are ready to fall with the slightest touch, the turn of a knob, a domestic treaty. It was all a huge mistake. I don't know who pulled the trigger. I don't know how late it is now. All I know is they all need to be saved from themselves. Maybe they all pulled the trigger. Maybe they all buried the body in the sub-basement. There was no way to know fire would reveal the past, a body like water, our future trembling like a divining rod. I sat down on the ghost of a chair and watched the sun rise like a basketball on fire, lit a cigarette for another house fire celebration. We all want to be anonymous.

Freaks

Seattle waterfront, three Indians sharing a bottle of wine and a can of Spam as I walk by. Me, the Indian tourist with half-braids and a wallet full of money.

"Hey, cousin," one of the Indians asks me. "Do you want a drink?"

"No thanks, cousin," I say and walk over to them.

"What tribe you are?" one of the Indians asks me. He's young, maybe twenty, but his nose is bright red with broken veins.

"Spokane," I say. "What tribe are you guys from?"

"I'm Lakota Sioux," the one with the red nose says, "And these two old farts are Yakima."

The two old Yakima look alike, almost twins.

"You guys are brothers, enit?" I ask.

They laugh hard.

"Shit, this is my son," the older Yakima says and he looks around two hundred years old. His son looks like he must be near one hundred and ninety-nine. Indian years are longer and harder even than dog years.

"Hey," I ask. "You guys need any change?"

"Yeah," red nose says. "A change of clothes, a change of underwear."

And we all laugh.

I pull out my wallet and give them a buck each. I don't feel generous or guilty, just half-empty and all lonely in this city which would kill me as slowly as it is killing these three cousins of mine.

"Thanks, brother," the Yakima son says and gives his dollar to his father. "My dad is the responsible one."

"What's your name?" red nose asks me.

"Victor. What are your names?"

"I'm Moe," red nose says. "And these guys are Larry and Curly."

And we laugh.

I say goodbye with handshakes and walk down the waterfront, passing by white tourists who don't care if they ever know my name. I walk all day, looking for just one more kind face.

Before We Knew About Mirrors

Disappearing Coins

Red Star, the hunchback magician, lived on the reservation in a one room house near the Catholic church. He was the man who could make his fingers disappear, transport quarters into the back pockets of Indian boys who suddenly believed in everything.

A quarter could be anything then: a jawbreaker, a piece of deer jerky from some grandmother, a Coke, a slice of the heart. But did Red Star pull those quarters from the air behind our hearts just to prove what we possessed in our chests, or did he take them from his own heart? Piece by piece, coin by coin, did he make himself, his dreams, less, every time a braided boy reached into a pocket?

I still have one of those quarters at the bottom of my coin jar, distinct and frightening in a sea of lesser pennies, nickels, dimes. What can I do to reach it? Spend, spend, find the smallest possible treasures in the dime stores, the garage sales, Goodwill? After I fill my small room with all that I've bought, will that quarter bring me any answers?

Pick a Card, Any Card

Indian boys always find some way to die. The faces I see in my mirror look the same: U.S. Government glasses, fractured nose, braids like wild ponies, eyes like mine and his and his and yours.

Everything we own, everything we want to own, is just that flat. Like slapping an open hand onto a table. Like pressing tightly against the walls. Like shuffling a deck of cards. But every card is the same, all face cards with the same face.

When an Indian stranger sees another Indian stranger, they both stare. They have the same eyes, mirrors, reflecting what they have witnessed; understanding the distance pain creates between past and present, they move toward random consolations.

So if someone hands us a card, calls it a dream, and asks if it's the correct one, what can we answer? Would we have time to baptize it, give it a Christian name, an education, the keys to a fast car? Will it be able to fancydance, anticipate the beating of drums, begin the message?

Rabbit from the Hat

Red Star the hunchback magician drank more than any of the Indians on the reservation. Assimilation, he called it, and meant it. Many mornings, we would find him passed out on the roadside, in a doorway, everywhere, and we would carry him home. Every morning, we would pull him up from the hole he'd thrown himself down the night before. Every morning, we would follow him down as he recanted years of his life.

"Indians can never live in the city."

"White women will break your heart."

"Money ain't worth shit."

"Never fall in love."

Red Star, you alcoholic wise man, none of your Indian boys ever fell in love.

Sawing Beautiful Women into Halves

Red Star the hunchback magician always said it was the only revenge that he ever had.

Levitation

Red Star the hunchback magician named us by the defects we possessed. I was Little Man, in town hat and hair, his favored assistant, gathering scarves, rings, coins, dreams.

I was the one levitating, supported by a single broomstick, always prepared to fall in some simple way.

I would close my eyes and dream of something strong, dream of horses exploding, rising into the air, their hearts beating survive, survive, survive.

Vanishing

The last time I saw Red Star the hunchback magician he was loading up a truck with everything he owned. All the boxes, rings, gimmicks, closets, where he kept all our future hidden.

"When you coming back?" I asked him.

"Never," he said and was gone.

Days later, we rummaged through his house, searching for answers. I found a book he'd left behind: *How to Fool and Amaze Your Friends: 101 Great Tricks of the Master Magicians*.

Red Star, you bastard, I know now how you did them all. I know everything.

Tiny Treaties

*And crying's like hating,
it won't ever pay. I'm going away
to where I'm from. I'm leaving,
last condor, last chance.*
—LORNA DEE CERVANTES

for Kari

I Would Steal Horses

I would steal horses
for you, if there were any left,
give a dozen of the best
to your father, the auto mechanic

in the small town where you were born
and where he will die in the dark.
I am afraid of his hands, which have
rebuilt more of the small parts

of this world than I ever will.
I would offer my sovereignty, take
every promise as your final lie, the last
point before we start refusing the exact.

I would wrap us both in old blankets
hold every disease tight against our skin.

Tiny Treaties

What I remember most about loving you
that first year is the December night
I hitchhiked fifteen miles through a blizzard
after my reservation car finally threw a rod
on my way back home from touching

your white skin again. Wearing basketball shoes
and a U.S. Army Surplus jacket
my hair long, unbraided, and magnified
in headlights of passing cars, trucks, two snowplows
that forced me off the road, escaping

into the dormant wheat fields. I laughed
because I was afraid but I wasn't afraid
of dying, just afraid of dying
in such a stupid manner. All the Skins
would laugh into their fists

at my wake. All the cousins would tell my story
for generations. I would be the perfect reservation metaphor:
a twentieth century Dull Knife
pulling his skinny ass and dreams
down the longest highway in tribal history.

What I imagine now
is the endless succession of white faces
hunched over steering wheels, illuminated
by cigarettes and dashboard lights, white faces
pressed against windows as cars passed by me

without hesitation. I waited seconds into years
for a brake light, that smallest possible treaty
and I made myself so many promises
that have since come true
but I never had the courage to keep

my last promise, whispered
just before I topped a small hill
and saw the 24-hour lights
of the most beautiful 7-11 in the world.
With my lungs aching, my hands and feet

frozen and disappearing, I promised
to ask if you would have stopped

and picked me up if you didn't know me
a stranger Indian who would have fallen in love
with the warmth of your car, the radio

and the steady rhythm
of windshield wipers over glass, of tires
slicing through ice and snow. I promised
to ask you that question every day
for the rest of our lives

but I won't ask you even
once. I'll just remain quiet
when memories of that first year
come roaring through my thin walls
and shake newspapers and skin.

I'll just wrap myself
in old blankets, build fires
from bald tires and abandoned houses
and I won't ask you the question
because I don't want to know the answer.

Spontaneous Combustion

Sometimes when an Indian boy loves
a white girl and vice versa

it's like waking up
with half of the world

on fire. You don't know
if you should throw water

onto those predictable flames
or let the whole goddamn thing burn.

Apologies

In his sleep, your father tears
at the skin rash he's been growing since World War II
when he ducked and covered
a few miles from Bikini Atoll. "Voluntary duty,"

he tells us. "I got to go home
a few months early." A half-century later
he curses the suggestion that we owe Japan
an apology for Nagasaki and Hiroshima. How is it

our own pain becomes feed
for anger, then fear and worst
a desperate logic
that justifies every piece of war? Memories

fall out from the attic
of history: the photograph
of a mummified Vietnamese soldier's skull
perched like a crazy ass scarecrow

on an American tank in '66 or '67
or whenever, this personal monument
designed by kids only minutes away
from high school football games. Of course

there is that other photograph
of another dark-skinned enemy, Bigfoot
the Minniconjou chief, frozen solid
in the snow at Wounded Knee, one hand

reaching toward the camera, a gesture
that would have looked staged today
but in 1876 it meant he died
with questions, but your father lives now

and you and I live now
together. All of us fake ceremonies
and feel dirty and used
when we wake too late

for a morning shower or watch
the evening news. *It's true.*
All day, we check our hair
in mirrors and mumble silent

apologies for the ordinary.
We say *Excuse me* to the fast food cashier
when our dollar bills are wrinkled
and *I'm sorry* to the tailor

measuring across our body
because of the proximity of our hearts.
Jesus, these apologies begin
with a whisper, then

become a war. Open your eyes
and force yourself out of bed
to face breakfast and work and the faces
of men and women who've been destroyed

by bullets and cocks and fists and hunger
just like all of us and none of us
because when it happens universally
it doesn't get noticed. So what to do?

Print up newspapers headlined PAIN
and bury all the apologies
in the classified ads? Raise money, dance
until exhaustion, drink, drugs, poetry?

I hate it all
and when your father curses the suggestion
that we owe the Japanese
any apology for Nagasaki and Hiroshima, I want

to tell him "It's all right
I understand" but I also want to strip him naked
and take photographs of his diseased skin
and I want to throw your father out the door

into the wheat fields, now snow fields
then killing fields. It happens that way:
violence changes the names of things.
Suddenly, at the STOP sign

I idle
in my car at the railroad crossing
as the train divides
the world into two halves: me

on this side with my predictable rage
and constant apologies
for the little things (I felt bad
this morning because I couldn't find the car keys)

and your father on the other side
singing loudest at church and storming
into silence when his heart is questioned.
Both of us love you

arrogantly and crazily, without apology.

Seven Love Songs Which Include the Collected History of the United States of America

And there are soldiers here
at the heart of things
but I don't know what wars
this love will bring.
—Lester FallsApart

1.

In this life, I feared you
                    more often
                    than I loved you
and made genetic excuses
for all of our mistakes

until even the ordinary wrapped itself in combustibles
and set the house on fire.

I blamed your arrogant grandfathers
for the flames and you
blamed my grandfathers
and their predictable anger.

Was it me who shot arrows
soaked in alcohol or was it you
who dropped another European match
without thought? We survived

only because of the hunger
strong as the falls we cross now
like ghosts of salmon.
                    We leap
from one generation

to the next.
My grandfathers and your grandfathers
would have hated each other, traded
only insults and gunfire

but we choose to love.

2.

After years of sleeping together, I still love
to stay up late
                    after you've passed into sleep

so I can hear you say things
you would never repeat
when awake. It's like loving two people, each
distinct and beautiful, as night from day
as you from me, all of us together forming

a continuous grace.

3.

After days
of fighting each other

we stop
call a truce
and retreat

down to Perkins 3rd Avenue
for breakfast.

As we waited to be seated
those familiar eyes stared
hateful and hurtful
from behind menus and newspapers

(but don't ask me
to explain those eyes
because any dark-skinned person knows
and every woman understands those eyes
that mean to kill)

and we endured the stares
until the entire restaurant was silent
and we finally left, angry
and bitter again. I shouted

"Must be asshole day in Perkins!"

as we walked out the door
but I realize now we should have stayed
sat down at the counter
exchanged tongue kisses
and fed each other

pancakes, pancakes, pancakes.

4.

Suddenly, we are all arms and legs
and it's summer and too hot to make love
but we do anyway on the kitchen floor
near the refrigerator with its door open.

It was not a movie; we were being practical.

5.

I was a fisherman for 15,000 years
before you stumbled onto my shore
your legs sea-heavy and awkward.

Do you remember?

How strange to know corn saved your life
but it's always the simple gifts that matter most.

So when I give you a can of commodity corn
instead of a dozen roses
it doesn't mean I don't love you
it means I want to save you

from hunger, disease, the long winter.
I can wrap you in old blankets
that smell like me

and I can hold you
with these hands
that held the spear,
that still hold the tribe

inches above the surface
of this river, this water

still and almost perfect, waiting
for the sudden
motion of arm, that strike
of stone into flesh.

We have learned that love is never civilized.

6.

In this dream I have, we are asleep together in a familiar bed. Maybe we are exhausted after a long day of work. Maybe we have been traveling long hours, driving all night down deserted highways with only the radio and our voices to keep us awake. But whatever the reason for our deep sleep, we don't hear the soldiers coming to take us away until it's too late. They blindfold us, drag us into unmarked cars and our families report us as missing. We join the ranks of the disappeared; we are buried separately after torture and interrogation. Maybe it was because you and I are African and drank from the wrong water fountain. Maybe it was because we are Japanese and built a better bridge across the Bering Strait. Maybe it was because we are Mexican and reinvented the horse. Maybe it was because we are both women and gave birth to the men who cut our throats. Maybe it was because we loved each other.

7.

But we always bring ourselves back
to beauty and grace. As now, when
I take your hand and we move in circles

that increase their diameter
with every word we share. This morning
you told me, "Maybe you should write a poem

about talking to people in an elevator
after it gets stuck between floors. Maybe
a nun, a man proud of his grandchildren,
an unemployed auto mechanic and a phlebotomist."

I told you then that no one would ever believe
all those people would be in the same elevator.
"But it's true," you said. "I shared an elevator
with all those people at the hospital today."

And we both laughed at the impossibility of all of it
at the impossibility of *us*. Who would ever believe
this story? If we translated our lives into every language
could we find an audience that understood the irony?

After 500 years of continuous lies
I would still sign treaties for you.

Watching Friends Sleep

1.

I give my bed up to friends who are tired after the long drive from Seattle, here to mend what I have made and not made of my life. Instead, they argue violently, glass is broken, skin bruised by rage. Neither is good enough for the other is what they argue, using logic that only love can create. They are beautiful and refuse to believe it. I wrap my arms around both, kiss separately and together until we all fall asleep. They, in my bed and me, on the floor. But it is too hot and uncomfortable for me so I lie awake, listen to my friends' hurried breathing and wonder if they are making love. I turn my head to watch but they are just dreaming. Of others? Of each other? They are dreaming in my bed and I think it would be good to hear them whisper and touch, to touch the blanket they push from the bed as they push against each other. It would be good to watch them, two shadows, two friends making love in my bed, filling those sheets and corners which have been empty now, since K left me. No. Since I left K. No. Empty now, for six days, which is, of course, all the time that it took God to create everything, anything, and I watch my friends sleep now. Amen, amen. Amen.

2.

Often, I lie
down on my bed
and pretend
to sleep, close
my eyes barely
and imagine
some story
or another, repeat
it the next day
to friends, swear
it was a dream
I woke from
terrified.

3.

Although I live miles and years from my reservation I sometimes dream of how hungry I used to be, how many nights I went to bed with nothing but sleep for dinner. Last night, I woke from another hungry dream and saw John eating crackers, watching television, and I forgot that my cupboards are now full, forgot that my refrigerator is filled with food that goes to waste sometimes, and I was angry with John for not sharing his crackers. I thought he had been hiding them from me. *I hate you,* I told John over and over and he said *Go back to sleep, you're dreaming.* Sometimes, it seems like it's too easy to forget when there was enough and too hard to remember anything but hunger, hunger, hunger.

4.

So eager to make his friends happy
Rod cooks a dinner
too expensive
for any of us to be eating
but we do eat
until our bellies protest
until our mouths hinge open
until Arthur pretends to be a salmon
and swims off to sleep
on the living room couch
until all of us fall
into various fetal positions
around the house
and Rod watches each of us
dream
his dinner all over again
wanting to make it last
beyond
our bodies.

5.

There are nights now when I wake from real nightmares and reach across the bed to touch my lover, long since departed. We've all done that, I know, we've all felt that absence as real as the absentee. But this is all new to me and sometimes it's *Fuck these memories* when they come and sometimes it's *Play some goddamn music so I can't hear myself breathe.* But anger was not to enter into this. Still, it's *Fuck these memories* when they haunt me and it's *Fuck these memories* when they refuse to let me leave the apartment to do laundry and it's *Fuck these memories* when I understand what they have come to mean and it's *Fuck these memories* when they force me to write poetry which can never be good enough. But anger was not to enter into this. My anger was not to enter into this. And once, Dick from Somerville called me up at 3 a.m. and said, "Metaphor is not real." So what's the use? I miss watching her sleep. That's all of it but it's not even close to what I mean.

Blankets

I have always loved sleeping
more
than I have ever loved
people

but that all changed when I slept with you. No. That all changed
after you left me and I discovered America was all about how
much I missed sleeping with you. Now, everything is different

even the blankets
I shared with you
in this bed
I said was just like the rest
of the world
because you, the white
flopped your arms and legs everywhere
and took all the room
and left me, the Indian
with just a small space
in the northwest corner

and now, sleeping alone, I have discovered America is too large,
too full of possibilities. Because of you, I sometimes believe the
Ghost Dancers were only half right. It's true we need the buffalo
back but we need the whites, too. At least, I need you

to cover me
like a good blanket
with warmth and faith,
I need you to cover me
like a smallpox blanket
with anger and pain.
I need you to cover me
like a tattered blanket
with fear and shame.
I need you to cover me
like a giveaway blanket
with honor and grace.

Gravity

We were bound, each
to our own planet

by gravity, by a love
that forced us

to orbit each other
so closely at times

we were aberrations
our moods changed

with every gesture:
turn of a key, flip

of a light switch.
So close, we nearly

collided and destroyed
everything. It's terrifying

I know, this release
now, from the other, one

become two, this
sudden change

in weight, size, dream.
I don't know

what hides behind
the last star

or even behind
the next star.

I only know
your stars, out

there, are white
and my stars, in

here, are red
and we'll arrive

at different destinations
separately.

Collect Calls

*This is AT&T with a collect call
from...Caller, what's your name?*

1.

My name is *Crazy Horse,* maybe it's *Neil Armstrong* or *Lee Harvey Oswald.* I am guilty of every crime; I was the first man on the moon. My name is repeated in dark rooms, at the bottom of stairways, behind umbrellas. My name is backmasked onto the soundtrack of my life.

2.

The soundtrack of my life: bat flapping against streetlight hanging over the basketball court; worn leather ball slapping pavement; horses; fry bread sizzle on the stove; steam exploding off hot sweatlodge rocks; *like a rhinestone cowboy;* gallon of tequila shattering on the road as Eugene loses his grip on the paper bag; powwow three in the morning drums; electric can opener; pine tree falling in the woods with nobody there to hear it; canned laughter; *one day at a time, sweet jesus;* mosquito buzz; old man coughing up a lifetime of nightmares at the breakfast table; cable television; absence of brakes as the pickup blasts through a guardrail; click of a lock; creak of hand closing into fist; knuckles popping; microwave changing its mind; *and I wonder what went wrong with our love;* busy signal.

3.

Busy signal. Busy signal. Busy signal. Operator, can I please speak to any Indian who lives in this city. Operator, just look for an Indian name in the directory, something obvious like Takes Enemy or Quick-to-See, any name you think could save me.

4.

You think you could save me from a history of three in the morning phone calls? At another pay phone I stand with empty pockets, all my change exhausted, calling the reservation collect, calling back 500 years of overdue bills. Once, in this apartment, I lay still and silent while generations of bill collectors pounded at my door. One needed cash for electricity; another wanted to repossess this English language I had rented to own. A desperate man placed ads in the local newspaper, had my photograph printed on the backs of milk cartons: *Have you seen this man?*

5.

This man I know was miles from home, hitchhiking toward San Francisco, when he disappeared. Seymour tells me this man could travel along telephone wire, burrow through recipes exchanged, tapdance over obscene phone calls, stagger around unrequited love. This man calls in the middle of the night, rings my phone until I answer, listens to me breathe, and then hangs up. Sometimes, he calls collect, calls from Pine Ridge, the Bering Sea, Gallup, Oz. He never leaves a name.

6.

Name? I don't know my name, operator, I was hoping you could tell me. Do you remember? Born from water into water with a spirit crushed by water, they told me to love my thirst. I hid in the outhouse and made friends with spiders; grass grew high and disguised my future. These possessions I remember: *Daredevil #3*, published in 1964, near-mint condition; 19-inch Quasar color television; U.S. Government glasses. Operator, I don't remember my area code, social security number, shoe size. Sometimes, in the dark, I hear voices calling out to me but they never use my name. Operator, do you remember?

7.

Remember, remember, remember, memory repeating like a scratched record. Lester FallsApart two-steps across the last Indian bar in Spokane. He stutters and staggers lyrics of the reservation song about the lover who left the bar and never came back. Spike told me every pay phone in the city was broken. *Tough shit guides our lives*. After closing, I climb into a taxicab and wake up years later at the bottom of a river.

8.

At the bottom of a river: your voice, salmontraveling by genetic memory and my heart, which could be a tire, waterlogged shoe, maybe the colored rock a child notices when he stands on the bridge and stares down into the clear water. Sweetheart, I am 15,000 years old and today your mother refused to accept my collect call.

9.

My collect call is misdirected, misplaced, and a phone rings at a pizza place in Beijing. *Do you deliver?* I ask, but they will only walk halfway across the Bering Sea. On waking, though, none of this is true. This vision arrived by accepting a collect call from a voice which named itself Truth and continued to lie, by a song which sang itself into an elevator of its own device. I was trapped between floors of a personal building, screaming into a red phone, hoping for rescue.

10.

Rescue me, operator, I'm standing at a pay phone on the Spokane Indian Reservation. A dozen stray dogs lean against the glass of the booth, their teeth white and frightening. Yes, operator, I know I'm only half a mile from home but there are so many obstacles along the way.

11.

Obstacles along the way: lions and tigers and bears; white whale; windmills; great white shark; Darth Vader; virginity; Hell's Angels; Canadian coins; Viet Cong; potholes; dueling banjos; Indians.

12.

Indians are living proof that nigger fuck buffalo. Do you remember, Indian boy, when your white friends taught you that song, sang it to you over the telephone?

13.

Over the telephone and through the woods into the reservation we go, in a '65 Malibu with four flat tires. Seymour tells me he's spent his whole life riding on the rims. Vernon calls his wife collect from a cellular phone we stole from a Cadillac in Spokane. How can anyone trace the calls if we keep on driving, if we're never in the same location for more than a moment?

14.

We're never in the same location for more than a moment. Movement is the soundtrack of my life; inertia is a busy signal. Operator, I know you love me but you can't save me from this man whose name I remember whenever I hear the river stopped, whenever he makes the collect call at three in the morning. He's the man who sniffs at my engine, kicks my tires, cleans the windshield so my vision will be perfect. He laughs when I offer him my last dollar bill as compensation, laughs when I drive into every obstacle along the way home. The man looks like a mirror with braids; the man laughs like a television set. Often, the battle on a reservation is Indians versus Indians and there are no reporters making telephone calls to editors with that story, reporting on winners and losers. There are no reporters dreaming headlines, no reporters and no witnesses.

Vision: From the Drum's Interior

Elvis Presley's Cadillac

Elvis Presley has left the stadium, has left the reservation 7-11. Arnold was working the graveyard shift when Elvis pulled up in a 1965 Mustang. "He threw down a handful of quarters for the pulltab machine," Arnold said. "He was humming some tune under his breath, something slow and easy." For days, the Indian boys debated about the exact song Elvis left in the 7-11, Maybe it was *Heartbreak Hotel*. Maybe it was *Love Me Tender*. Maybe it was *Jailhouse Rock*. Morris Medicine tells us he has Elvis Presley's pink cadillac FOR SALE, toward the debt Indian boys acquired by selling their turquoise dreams like roadside souvenirs. "Who was he?" asks Lester FallsApart. "Elvis was a poor white boy," I tell him. "He was trash. He was the dumpster singer who faked guitar and sang black music like it was his." Lester says, "Sounds like Elvis was making treaties in 4/4 time."

John Coltrane Blowing

If you listen tight you can hear a night train, if you listen tight you can hear John Coltrane blowing a "tender tenor pain" for the Indian boys to feel in their fingers and thumbs, the Indian boys feel it in their fingers and thumbs when they put hands to drums or to B-7 on the reservation jukebox Saturday night. Coltrane has been B-7 on the jukebox every night since the beginning, long before our salmon ladders and electricity, before salmon ladders and random electricity threw the Indian boy into the city where he put his ear to the cold pavement of streets, pressed his ear against the moist street and hear the drumbeat of a reservation train bringing back the answer, a Coltrane blowing out reasons for a fancydancer.

20th Century Fancydancing

Who said, "I figured drums was my best defense?" Who said, "I am in the reservation of my mind?" Was it Toni and Adrian who heard drums in words? I want to fancydance back into the reservation of my mind, fancydancing toward a vision, a 20th century measure of music, music of commodity cans and six-packs, music of stickgames: forgiveness hidden in the hands of old Indian women who need you to choose the hand holding our future tight. "Is it the left or the right hand?" Both fancydance easily at the ends of arms which held you as hard as they ever held this drum or any other drum. It's the drum, yes, the reservation is a drum, the music beyond *Love Me Tender,* the music just before *A*

73

Love Supreme, drums pulling you fast from your skinny bed at 3 a.m. from dreams you barely remember, dreams echoing through the reservation night air, where you stood once at the window of the largest HUD house in the world, waiting for the music of the powwow to finish before you went back to sleep, knowing drums would button your shirt, tie your shoes, open the front door and throw you back onto the road, back into the river, changing the current as you stand in the middle of a new life, new music for the 20th century fancydancer fancydancing. *Fancydancing.*

How to Obtain Eagle Feathers for Religious Use

for G.S.

*The Federal law protecting bald and golden eagles
makes provisions for the use of eagle feathers by
Native Americans for religious purposes.*
—U.S. Government Bulletin

Page 1

Picture an eagle or parts of an eagle. That has nothing to do
with it. Remember: I am the Indian who wrote the obituary for the
obituary editor and have come to know these things. Often, I have
stood in places where nothing has happened. For instance, the
summer I worked forestry for the BIA and found a strand of
barbed wire fence still nailed to a pine tree. Stapled to the barbed
wire was a hand-painted sign: NO TRESPASSING. INDIAN LAND.
1876. I have no memory of the artist.

Page 9

An Indian plays piano somewhere on the reservation when we
close our eyes to sleep. The song is familiar, something close to
Elvis before he grew fat, useless. Believe us: an Indian waits by
the dumpster outside the trading post. He swears he is Elvis in
braids. He wears feathers and Levis. We give him a quarter or two
every time we go to the store. Soon, it will be enough.

Index

Arrowheads and Alcohol, BIA and Basketball, Commodities and
Clear Cut, Department of Interior and Dogs, Errors and Eagles,
Forgiveness and Fancydancing, Gasoline and God, Hell and
Heroes, Indians and Ignorance, Jerky and Jumpshots, Keno and
Kerosene, Love and Lust, Mothers and Madmen, Necklaces and
Notebooks, Orgasms and Oranges, Porcupines and Playing Cards,
Quilts and Quotas, Roaches and Receiving Docks, Sin and
Sunburn, Terror and Towels, Underarms and Underachievers,
Victories and Variables, Weed and Wonder, X-Rays and X-Rated,
Yesterday and Youth, Zeroes and Zip Codes.

Page 7

*Applications for a permit to acquire eagle feathers for religious
use may be made by completing the* macaroni & cheese dinner, by
opening the bag of commodity noodles, by shredding the com-
modity cheese, by pulling the cast-iron pot down from the shelf,

by boiling water and adding a pinch of salt, by paying the light bill, by renting the HUD house, by working for the BIA, by running the four-minute mile.

Rough Draft

All of this is excellent, Stan, but where's the human interest angle? How many parts of an eagle equals one eagle? Also, what is the average number of feathers per eagle? Does the bald eagle have fewer feathers than the golden? Goddammit, Stan, it's like asking someone to hand you a piano. Which came first, Christopher Columbus or the eagle?

Page 5

Photograph: an Indian with a stoic face. No, he's brown-skinned and smiles, holds a flashlight above his head. No, it's an eagle or parts of an eagle. But none of this has anything to do with it. There is a photograph of another Indian, not a totally different man, but different enough to make the two photos separate. This other Indian in the photograph is holding a flashlight. He is not smiling. He walks slowly through the powwow grounds and searches for something. What is it? What is it?

End Notes

Do you remember the eagles who came to Little Falls Dam every summer? Yes, they came the summer we went to Disneyland. Every Spokane Indian climbed into cars, trucks, wagons, and traveled north to the Magic Kingdom, leaving the eagles alone at Little Falls Dam. I was locked in the trunk of a '65 Malibu and no one let me out until all the complimentary tickets were gone. Lester FallsApart is still there, going crazy in a tea cup. Revolution after revolution, he continues, past history and the television's uninterrupted news. Picture an eagle or parts of an eagle. *It will not be enough for the twenty-first century.*

The Native American Broadcasting System

But Y holds the fly swatter,
The Doomsday Weapon, and the deed to X's land.
—DONNA BROOK

for Paula & Marina

On The Amtrak From Boston To New York City

The white woman across the aisle from me says, "Look,
look at all the history, that house
on the hill there is over two hundred years old,"
as she points out the window past me

into what she has been taught. I have learned
little more about American history during my few days
back East than what I expected and far less
of what we should all know of the tribal stories

whose architecture is 15,000 years older
than the corners of the house that sits
museumed on the hill. "Walden Pond,"
the woman on the train asks, "Did you see Walden Pond?"

and I don't have a cruel enough heart to break
her own by telling her there are five Walden Ponds
on my little reservation out West
and at least a hundred more surrounding Spokane,

the city I pretend to call my home. "Listen,"
I could have told her. "I don't give a shit
about Walden. I know the Indians were living stories
around that pond before Walden's grandparents were born

and before his grandparents' grandparents were born.
I'm tired of hearing about Don-fucking-Henley saving it, too,
because that's redundant. If Don Henley's brothers and sisters
and mothers and fathers hadn't come here in the first place

then nothing would need to be saved."
But I didn't say a word to the woman about Walden
Pond because she smiled so much and seemed delighted
that I thought to bring her an orange juice

back from the food car. I respect elders
of every color. All I really did was eat
my tasteless sandwich, drink my Diet Pepsi
and nod my head whenever the woman pointed out

another little piece of her country's history
while I, as all Indians have done
since this war began, made plans
for what I would do and say the next time

somebody from the enemy thought I was one of their own.

The Game Between the Jews and the Indians is Tied Going Into the Bottom of the Ninth Inning

So, now, when you touch me
my skin, will you think
of Sand Creek, Wounded Knee?
And what will I remember

when your skin is next to mine
Auschwitz, Buchenwald?
No, we will only think of the past
as one second before

where we are now, the future
just one second ahead
but every once in a while
we can remind each other

that we are both survivors and children
and grandchildren of survivors.

Because I Was In New York City Once
And Have Since Become An Expert

for Rosa

The basketball rims had no nets, not even chains, so every shot was a matter of *knowing* how it felt when it left the hand. Just as they let go of the ball shooters called *point* or *rebound* and played from there, adding one to the score or running back on defense.

But I watched all that happen from the car as we drove by outdoor courts where every player had darker skin than mine. Everyone walking past me, through me, in the streets, on the subway, had darker skin.

I had been Native American all my life and now I was Chicano, Puerto Rican, Chinese, Japanese, Iraqi, a non-practicing Jew.

No one told me I should have learned to say *I don't speak your language* in forty-seven different tongues.

Walking down the aisles of the pharmacy across the street from Lincoln Center—the white clerk didn't watch me closely, expecting me to shoplift. For that, I almost missed Spokane, the city where I was born and which reminds me continually of my dark eyes and hair and skin.

Could it be true? Am I Native American only when I am hated because of it? Does racism determine my entire identity?

Once, I stepped out in front of traffic, oblivious for a second to how little we all care about each other, and only Bob's quick hands saved me from *what?*

I, who once believed he knew so much about survival, found out that he didn't always recognize the enemy. But, when that taxicab roared by an inch from me, I could see that driver's face and he looked like Custer in a turban.

Still, there is beauty in everything.

Stopped at a red light, I looked out the window to see a man in a suit buy a slice of pizza from a sidewalk vendor. Then the man in the suit dropped his briefcase so he set the pizza down on the cart. As he bent down to pick up his briefcase, a stray dog came running out of nowhere, maybe from the Spokane Indian Reservation, and jumped into the air over the food cart, snatched the pizza off the paper plate and ran down the block.

The man in the suit cursed wildly as the dog raced away. But the dog stopped suddenly, turned around, and came running back at the man in the suit. That man wasn't cursing now, he had visions of rabies and scar tissue. Then, the dog jumped into the air again, snatched the paper plate from the cart, and raced off down the other way.

All the while I was thinking *What manners that dog has!* All the while I was thinking *Good dog, good dog, good dog.*

The Native American Broadcasting System

1.

Five hundred years from now, archaeologists will discover
a bowling ball buried beside the body of an Indian chief.

Research papers will be published in the academic journals prov-
ing the existence of a large fifteen-pound globe-like organ
in a majority of late twentieth century Native Americans.

"Although the organ itself was petrified," states an expert,
"We were able to ascertain that its purpose was to absorb excess
quantities of fluids, most likely alcoholic in nature."

2.

NEWS BULLETIN: The American Academy of Motion Picture Arts
and Sciences has announced the establishment of a new category
for this year's Academy Awards: Best Performance by a Non-
Native in a Native American Role. Nominees this year include Burt
Lancaster, Charles Bronson, Trevor Howard, Burt Reynolds, and
Kevin Costner.

3.

The reservation penny still lying on the ground
        with no Indian left around
to bend down and pick it up and it's a buffalo
        penny (what a coincidence)
so when you flip it, chances are even
        you'll still see Lincoln.
So what's left but to leave the damn thing
        where it belongs, under
our feet, collecting dust, sticking to the bare feet
        of Indian children who don't
have any shoes, socks, or even the smallest wet dream?

4.

Baby, come make me promises, come
close and whisper to me of land claims
uranium mines and tax-free cigarettes.
Baby, hold my hand when we cross the Spokane River
into the United States of America, kiss me
in the dark, fuck me against the back wall of a 7-11.

5.

Custer came back to life in Spokane managing the Copper Penny Grocery, stocked the rubbing alcohol next to the cheap wine:

RUBBING ALCOHOL 99¢
THUNDERBIRD WINE $1.24

The urban Indians shuffle in with tattered coats and boots, counting quarters while Custer trades food stamps for cash, offering absolution.

6.

The old man on the Greyhound asks me why
so many Indians ride the bus. I tell him
it's about loneliness, all about loneliness.

The old man on the Greyhound asks me if
I know what that word means. I tell him
it's the sound of glass breaking, dust
from smallpox blankets filling the lungs
horses exploding beneath wheels, houses
swallowing up all the cold air, children
running bareback through barbed wire, hearts
pounding under glass in the pawn shop.

The old man on the Greyhound asks me where
I've been, where I'm going. I tell him
I just got back from pissing in the Atlantic
and I'm traveling to the exact edge
of the West to piss in the Pacific.
Everybody has to have a mission.

7.

NEWS BULLETIN: Thirteen heavily armed Native Americans stormed the beach at Liberty Island today and inverted the Statue of Liberty.

8.

And where do we go from here? All I know
        is that I hide myself in
Lester FallsApart's right shoe, waiting
        for the next General Assistance
check, cussing at all the Indians passed out
        half-assed awake, listening
and believing that Lester's goddamn right shoe
        can talk, can make campaign

promises, invent slogans, report baseball scores
        the weather, the father who
killed his family with a spoon, knife, and two forks.

9.

I am the essence of powwow, I am
toilets without paper, I am fry bread
in sawdust, I am bull dung
on rodeo grounds at the All-Indian
Rodeo and Horse Show, I am

the essence of powwow, I am
video games with braids, I am spit
from toothless mouths, I am turquoise
and bootleg whiskey, both selling
for twenty bucks a swallow, I am

the essence of powwow, I am
fancydancers in flannel, I am host drum
amplified, I am *Fuck you*
don't come back and *Leave me*

the last hard drink. I am
the essence of powwow, I am the dream
you lace your shoes with, I am
the lust between your toes, I am
the memory you feel across the bottom
of your feet whenever you walk too close.

10.

NEWS BULLETIN: The Adolph Coors Corporation is sponsoring a
new promotional contest. On the bottom inside of every beer can
and bottle, Coors had printed a single letter. The first Indian to
collect and spell out the word RESERVATION will receive a train
ticket for a special traveling back 555 years.

11.

Buffalo Bill came back to life and hunted pianos.
During a period of roughly 25 years, he shot 3 million
pianos west of the Mississippi alone. An old-timer
remembers the summer he was trapped on a boulder

on the plains when the Great Northern Piano Herd
passed by him. There were pianos as far as the eye
could see, pianos upon pianos, all wild and within
an arm's length, pianos from horizon to horizon.

12.

There could be a global nuclear war
        and the last white man
left alive would convince himself he was Cherokee
        and would travel from
monument to monument, reinventing his own personal
        Trail of Tears, invite his feet
to stomp a new and improved dust down into
        the ground, print up a T-shirt
advertising it all for nobody: the First Annual
        All-Indian, Six-Foot-and-Under
45-Years-and-Over Trail of Tears Revisited.

13.

Baby, don't leave me in the in-between, between
window panes, I-90 and Highway 2, red and white
cash and credit, here and there, this and that
treaty and Sand Creek, between Thunderbird wine
and rubbing alcohol, artificial turf and grass
the dreams you save and the dreams you pawn.
Baby, don't leave me in the in-between, between
the bilateral symmetries of love and lust.

14.

Don't judge a man until you've walked a mile
        in his moccasins, you call it corn
we call it maize, don't litter or Iron Eyes Cody
        will shed a solitary tear
do as the great Indian chiefs of the past
        and leave everything
the way you found it but nobody loves a drunken Indian
        anger in his heart, bitter
and more than a little confused, give him a uniform
        a medal from Iwo Jima, a flag
folded into a box, give him a pair of combat boots
        so damn big he can use them
as a foxhole, give him a pair of Army socks so dry
        and tight and white they never
get themselves dirty, give him a book on survival
        and cut out the last chapter
give him a pair of glasses that reflect back so he can
        only see his eyes lying
again, give him a parade through the reservation
        so the Indian children will finally

receive their visions, give him a blind horse
    who isn't afraid of trees
give him a car without brakes or a steering wheel
    give him a ticket to the symphony
and tell him all the flutes are snakes, give him
    a basketball and tell him
to play his way off the reservation, give him a manual
    for home improvement
without a table of contents, steal all his hammers
    and nails, give him keys
to a door, a door that don't belong to no house.

15.

Baby, come make me promises, tell me
you'll love me as long as
the winds blow
the grasses grow
the rivers flow.

Split Decisions

Float like a butterfly,
sting like a bee.

1.

Memory: Muhammad Ali
                    knocked down
for the first time
in his career
by a thunderous left hook
                    from Joe Frazier.

He had so many reasons
to stay
down.

2.

Stay down! Stay down! I imagine
                    Muhammad Ali
heard every voice, felt
every pair of white hands
pressed down against his chest

white hands
reaching through the television set.

3.

On closed circuit television in the Spokane Coliseum, I watched
Muhammad Ali hit the canvas with the weight of 500 years on his
chest. Joe Frazier and most of the audience went to a neutral cor-
ner but my father and I needed Ali to rise, needed him to justify
the $50 we had spent on the tickets when there wasn't enough
food in the house, needed him to justify why we ignored the $200
offer to scalp the tickets to a desperate white man outside the
Coliseum, but there were so many reasons for Ali to stay down.

4.

Downstream
from the bridge in Louisville
Cassius Clay's Olympic Gold Medal

waits
at the bottom
of the river.

In 1964, this country needed
and loved Cassius Clay.

5.

But this country didn't need or love Muhammad Ali. When he fell to the canvas, down for the first time in his life, an entire country wanted to count him out. Muhammad Ali, the Black man who stood up and said *I won't fight in Vietnam. I ain't got no quarrel with those Viet Cong.* Ali stood up in defense of all of us and didn't run. He leaned back against the ropes, *rope-a-dope,* and took the insane right hook of Uncle Sam. They stripped his title, stole his money, and sent him into exile for three years. A white champion would have playfully sparred with Bob Hope in a USO show. Did anyone call Ali a hero?

6.

My
heroes
carry
guns
in
their
minds.

7.

Win their hearts and minds and we win the war.

Can you hear that song echo
across history? This country couldn't win
Muhammad Ali's heart and mind
so they made him into another dark-skinned enemy.

8.

Children, the enemy reads us
                    the news
at 6 o'clock every night.

9.

Nightfall equals MC^2 in Mississippi.

Nightfall is the moon rising according to social class.

Nightfall is a BLACKOUT in New York City.
(Does that mean electricity is European?)

Nightfall is the punchline to Muhammad Ali falling
to the canvas after a Joe Frazier left hook.

10.

Joe Frazier punched Ali so hard to the body
he pissed blood after the fight.

That didn't make Ali a hero.

When he was down on the canvas, floored
by a textbook hook from Frazier
did Ali have time and mind to think?

He had never lost a fight
and there he was, on closed circuit television
broadcast to most of the planet
and he was down
         for the first time

in his whole life. Did he have time
to think about the pain of his broken
         jaw?

Years later, in 1991, I see him in the ring
again on cable television, a special guest
introduced before a heavyweight championship fight.

Battling Parkinson's disease, he barely raises
his arms above eye level
when the ring announcer shouts his name.

What did Muhammad Ali do to deserve this?

11.

What have we done to deserve these kind of heroes? Where is the
national holiday for Muhammad Ali? Where is the poetry? Carolyn
tells me Ali wrote his own poetry but I've never seen it dancing
beside the words of any other hero. Muhammad Ali's poetry
floated like a butterfly and stung like a bee. *We should all write
exactly that way.*

12.

There is no other way to say this:

when the camera closed in on Muhammad Ali
in 1991, his eyes clouded
                    by fear and disease

I needed and loved him
beyond what I knew

needed him to be a hero again. In my mind
I traveled back to that night
when Joe Frazier knocked Ali down
with a thunderous left hook.

Ali was down inside the ring
while millions of us stood
on the outside
                    watching and waiting.

13.

I
am
waiting
for
someone
to
tell
the
truth.

14.

It's true the African American is a better fighter than the European
American because he has to spend his whole life fighting. It's true
this country doesn't stop punching when the bell rings.

15.

When the bell rang at the end of the fight
after Joe Frazier had floored Ali with a left hook
you must remember that Muhammad Ali was still standing

he stood up.

Citizens

Lee Harvey Oswald

I went deer hunting with Lee Harvey Oswald down near Little Falls, just inside the reservation border. I swear to you that even when he mustered up enough courage to pull the trigger, he never came close to any of the deer we saw that day. When I saw his face all over the papers the next day, I looked out the window and saw this big black truck roll by, loaded up with all these dead deer. *Poachers,* I thought first but then I saw the men in the cab of the pickup wore three-piece suits, sunglasses, and had little earphones stuck in their ears. I told Seymour what I saw and he shook his head at me and said *This reservation is exactly like Dallas.* But I didn't believe him until I saw George Armstrong Custer rise from the grave and shoot Lee Harvey Oswald in the stomach on national television. I still have the news clipping, that front page photo, taped to my refrigerator. Every time I go to get a beer or slice of commodity cheese, I see it. I've seen it all. I saw who stood behind that fence on the Grassy Knoll. I saw who pulled that trigger. Believe me, that man behind the fence smoked tax-free cigarettes and had beautiful braids.

Patsy Cline

Before the old Tribal School was condemned, I swear Patsy Cline used to sing there after lights went out at the end of the day. After the old Tribal School was condemned, I swear Patsy Cline sang continuously, night after night. Our HUD house was right across the street from the old Tribal School and maybe I was the only one who heard her. More likely, I was the only one who would admit it. Even though Indians still believe and practice magic, there ain't a medicine woman or man alive who would've been able to figure out why Patsy Cline would be singing in the old Tribal School. And me, I've got even less magic than the ordinary Indian, so all I can do is lie in my bed and listen. Believe me, Patsy Cline is here on my reservation, walking after midnight, searching. Just like me. Just like you.

Robert DeNiro

I used to think he lived on my reservation in that green house on the hill, near the water tower. Not because I ever saw him or even imagined I saw him. Only because every light in the house was always on and the car that sat in the driveway moved so gradually that it took me a year to realize it. Like a clock, the car pointed north, pointed toward twelve on New Year's Day. By the time summer ended, the car pointed south toward six. At Christmas, it was nearly at twelve again. I knew only Robert DeNiro could get away with something that crazy and exact. I knew only Robert DeNiro could test my tribe's edges like that and not push us completely over. I knew only Robert DeNiro could afford the electricity bill.

Sittin' On The Dock Of the Bay

Otis Redding
died only a few days after

he recorded his last song.
Otis Redding died

only three days after he sang
his last song. I want it

to happen that way
for me. I want to die

only after I've written
that last poem, those words

which might finally define
what I've called my life, spent

sitting on the dock
of Benjamin Lake, half the time

swatting reservation mosquitoes
interested in my Indian blood only

the other half staring down
into the water at faces

of the three Indians who drowned
here during my lifetime:

one by accident, one on purpose
one because there was nothing else to do.

Rediscovering America

Scene 1

Drums. Nearly deafening. They fade out and are replaced by the slight sound of country and western music, something like Hank Williams. Something like *I'm So Lonesome, I Could Cry*. Lester FallsApart, Suzy Boyd, and Seymour sit together at a table in the center of the stage. The Bartender and the Waitress argue violently, each on either side of an imaginary bar, at stage left. Suddenly, the Bartender throws a real beer mug (empty) through the air, above Lester, Suzy, and Seymour, off stage where it shatters very loudly.

Off Stage

Christopher Columbus staggers, holds his hands to his bleeding head. Lester comes running from on stage, visibly excited. "Damn," Lester yells. "That was beautiful. Did you see that, Seymour? Did you hear that, Suzy? That damn bartender is the Dizzy Dean of the reservation, the Sandy Koufax for the alcoholic, the Cy Young of broken glass. Damn, that's so fucking tragic it's like another treaty." Christopher Columbus falls to the floor, bleeding profusely. Three emergency medical technicians wearing braids and Levi's rush in from on stage, carrying various medical supplies. "This is no good," one EMT says to the other two. "We have to get him to the clinic." An Indian Health Service ambulance drives in from on stage and the three EMTs load Christopher Columbus into it, just before the ambulance reverses quickly, lights flashing, backs on stage.

Scene 2

The three EMTs in braids and Levis wheel Christopher Columbus into the Indian Health Service clinic, followed closely by Lester. As they wheel Christopher Columbus into an examining room, all the Native American employees shout in unison: "Christopher Columbus, you've found us!" Nine white doctors rush into the room, all in white T-shirts with DOCTOR printed in black letters on their chests. There is confusion, near panic, until the tallest doctor shouts, "X-rays! We need X-rays!" Everyone runs out the door, except Lester and Christopher Columbus. The two stare at each other silently for a moment and then turn their heads to face the audience and/or us.

Tableau

Lester opens his mouth wide and lets out a silent war cry. He is a method actor, so imagines, even places himself, riding a pony on the Great Plains, circa 1876. Suddenly, Lester is dressed in full traditional wardance outfit, with the addition of mirrored sunglasses and high-top basketball shoes. Lester dances around Christopher Columbus, still bleeding. Then, the image blurs, melts, and we are left with the white noise of an empty screen.

Intermission

The lights come on in the theater and all the white people in the audience cry out and cover their eyes. The solitary Indian man in the back row smiles. He is wearing mirrored sunglasses. White people panic, rush for exits blindly, crushing each other to death. There is a sense of complete suffocation. Two teenagers in the balcony still kiss passionately. A fat man in a suit refuses to let go of his popcorn. The usher adjusts the thermometer. Then, the house lights go dark, the screen blasts an image in black and white. It's Lee Marvin in a lifeboat, taking control.

Ship of Fools

Lee Marvin sprays saliva as he shouts at the dozen people clinging weakly to survival, to the only lifeboat in the Pacific and/or Atlantic Ocean. Lee Marvin holds a small dog tight to his chest as he yells, "Goddamn it, people, there are too many of you on board! One of you has to jump to save the rest!" On board: the beautiful young schoolteacher with an armful of math exams, ungraded; the autoworker who stares sullenly into the camera; Joey, the adolescent with the troubled past; the aging movie star clutching a tarnished Academy Award; the young middle-class couple in the process of confessing their extramarital affairs; the handsome, if somewhat feminine, bachelor weeping quietly; the elderly couple who will jump into the ocean together if it comes to that; the crew cut military man traveling home on leave; the mysterious diplomat with a briefcase handcuffed to his wrist; the pregnant woman with a life insurance policy. "Listen, please," Lee Marvin pleads now. "One of you has to go over. Whoever has served mankind the least." The lifeboat shudders, the ocean boils, the small dog barks. Then, Lee Marvin points a long finger at the one he has chosen. "You," Lee Marvin whispers. "You will go over." As the camera pans over the moist faces, the film goes black, replaced sharply by the interior of a bar. Seymour and Suzy sit alone at a table while the Bartender and the Waitress argue violently near the front door.

Scene 3

Suzy stands suddenly, reaches for Seymour. "Do you want to dance?" Seymour takes her hand and they lead each other out to the dance floor. The jukebox plays something stolen, something tender. Seymour and Suzy hold each other tight, dancing a two-step. As the music fades, they stare into each other's eyes, smile slightly and kiss. The image dissolves, replaced by screen credits, the copyright, and then silence. The audience applauds politely, leaves the theater and drives home.

The Tonight Show

Arriving home, you switch on the television. The Tonight Show with Johnny's guest host, Christopher Columbus. Still wearing an ace bandage wrapped around his head, he introduces his first guest as "a talented new stand-up comedian, Lester FallsApart." Lester fumbles through those huge curtains as the studio audience remains completely silent. Lester kicks the microphone over, stands half in and half out of the spotlight. He clears his throat loudly and opens his mouth to speak.

Captivity

He (my captor) gave me a biscuit, which I put in my pocket, and not daring to eat it, buried it under a log, fearing he had put something in it to make me love him.

—from the narrative of Mrs. Mary Rowlandson, who was taken captive when the Wampanoag destroyed Lancaster, Massachusetts, in 1676.

1.

When I tell you this story, remember it may change: the reservation recalls the white girl with no name or a name which refuses memory. October she filled the reservation school, this new white girl, daughter of a BIA official or doctor in the Indian Health Service Clinic. Captive, somehow afraid of the black hair and flat noses of the Indian children who rose, one by one, shouting their names aloud. She ran from the room, is still running, waving her arms wildly at real and imagined enemies. Was she looking toward the future? Was she afraid of loving all of us?

2.

All of us heard the explosion when the two cars collided on the reservation road. Five Indians died in the first car; four Indians died in the second. The only survivor was a white woman from Springdale who couldn't remember her name.

3.

I remember your name, Mary Rowlandson. I think of you now, how necessary you have become. Can you hear me, telling this story within uneasy boundaries, changing you into a woman leaning against a wall beneath a HANDICAPPED PARKING ONLY sign, arrow pointing down directly at you? Nothing changes, neither of us knows exactly where to stand and measure the beginning of our lives. Was it 1676 or 1976 or 1776 or yesterday when the Indian held you tight in his dark arms and promised you nothing but the sound of his voice? September, Mary Rowlandson, it was September when you visited the reservation grade school. The speech therapist who tore the Indian boy from his classroom, kissed him on the lips, gave him the words which echoed treaty: *He thrusts his fists against the posts but still insists he sees the ghosts.* Everything changes. Both of us force the sibilant, in the language of the enemy.

4.

Language of the enemy: *heavy lightness,* house insurance, *serious vanity,* safe-deposit box, *feather of lead,* sandwich man, *bright smoke,* second-guess, *sick health,* shell game, *still-waking sleep,* forgiveness.

5.

How much longer can we forgive each other? Let's say I am the fancydancer and every step is equal to a drum beat, this sepia photograph of you and me staring into the West of our possibilities. For now, you are wearing the calico dress that covers your ankles and wrists and I'm wearing a bone vest wrapped around a cotton shirt, my hair unbraided and unafraid. This must be 1876 but no, it is now, August, and this photograph will change the story. Remember: I am not the fancydancer, am not the fancydancer, not the fancydancer, the fancydancer, fancydancer.

6.

Fancydance through the tall grass, young man, over broken glass, past Crowshoe's Gas Station where you can buy an Indian in a Bottle. "How do you fit that beer-belly in there?" asks a white tourist. "We do it," I tell her, "piece by piece."

7.

Piece by piece, I reassemble the house where I was born, but there is a hole in the wall where there was none before. "What is this?" I ask my mother. "It's your sister," she answers. "You mean my sister made that hole?" "No," she says. "That hole in the wall is your sister." For weeks, I searched our architecture, studied the walls for imperfections. Listen: imagination is all we have as defense against capture and its inevitable changes.

8.

I have changed my mind. In this story there are words fancydancing in the in-between, between then and now, between walls in the alley behind the Tribal Cafe where Indian boys smoke old cigarettes at halftime of the all-Indian basketball game. Mary Rowlandson, it's true, isn't it? Tobacco and sugar are the best weapons.

9.

The best weapons are the stories and every time the story is told, something changes. Every time the story is retold, something changes. There are no photographs, nothing to be introduced as evidence. The 20th century overtook the reservation in 1976, but there we were, stuck in 1975. Do you remember that white boy then, who spent the summer on the reservation? I don't know how he arrived. Did his father pilot a DC-10 forced to make an emergency landing in the Trading Post parking lot? Did the BIA Forestry man find him frozen in amber? Did Irene sweep him up from the floor of a telephone booth? Lester FallsApart says he himself drank and half-swallowed the white boy out of a bottle of Annie Green Springs wine and spat him out whole into the dust. The nightwatchman at the Midnight Mine tells us he caught the white boy chewing uranium. Do you remember that white boy dove naked into Benjamin Lake? He wore the same Levi's hung low on the hips, a red bandanna wrapped around his head. He tugged at his blond hair, yes, telling us "It will grow, I promise." We beat him often, specifically. Arnold broke the white boy's nose with a snowball he had saved, frozen and hidden in the fridge since March. It was July 4th when we kidnapped him and kept him captive in a chicken coop for hours. We spat and pissed on him through the wire; Seymour shot him twice with a pellet gun. That white boy fell backward into the nests, crushed eggs, splintered wood, kicked chickens blindly. I was the first to stop laughing when the white boy started digging into dirt, shit, the past, looking for somewhere to hide. We did not make him any promises. He was all we had left.

10.

All we had left was held captive here on the reservation, Mary Rowlandson, and I saw you there chewing salmon strips in the corner, hiding from all the Indians. Did you see him, Mary Rowlandson, the Indian man who has haunted your waking for 300 years, who left you alone sipping coffee in the reservation 7-11? I saw you there, again, as I walked home from the bar, grinning to the stars, but all you could do was wave from the window and mouth the eternal question: *How?*

11.

How do you open a tin can without a sharp-edged dream? How do you sleep in your post office box using junk mail for blankets? How do you see past the iron bars someone painted on your U.S. government glasses? How do you stop a reservation tsunami before it's too late?

12.

It's too late, Mary Rowlandson, for us to sit together and dig up the past you buried under a log, salvage whatever else you had left behind. What do you want? I cannot say, "I love you. I miss you." June, Mary Rowlandson, the water is gone and my cousins are eating Lysol sandwiches. They don't need you, will never search for you in the ash after your house has burned to the ground one more time. It's over. That's all you can depend on.

13.

All we can depend on are the slow-motion replays of our lives. Frame 1: Lester reaches for the next beer. Frame 2: He pulls it to his face by memory, drinks it like a 20th century vision. Frame 3: He tells a joke, sings another song: *Well, they sent me off to boarding school and made me learn the white man's rules.*

14.

White man's rules: all of us must follow them, must remember the name of the officer who arrested us for running when the sign said DON'T WALK. It's the language of the enemy. There is no forgiveness for fancydancing on WET CEMENT. Before we move into the HUD house, we must build dreams from scratch, piece by piece, because SOME ASSEMBLY IS REQUIRED. Remember to insert CORRECT CHANGE ONLY when you choose the best weapons, the stories which measure all we have left. How do you know whether to use the IN or OUT door to escape? But it's too late to go now, our four-door visions have been towed from a NO PARKING ZONE. Leonard tells me he's waiting for the bus to the dark side of the moon, or Oz, or the interior of a drum. I load up my pockets with all my possessions and wait with him. That Greyhound leaves at 3 a.m. That's all we can depend on.

My Heroes Have Never Been Cowboys

1.

In the reservation textbooks, we learned Indians were invented in 1492 by a crazy mixed-blood named Columbus. Immediately after class dismissal, the Indian children traded in those American stories and songs for a pair of tribal shoes. *These boots are made for walking, babe, and that's just what they'll do. One of these days these boots are gonna walk all over you.*

2.

Did you know that in 1492 every Indian instantly became an extra in the Great American Western? But wait, I never wondered what happened to Randolph Scott or Tom Mix. The Lone Ranger was never in my vocabulary. On the reservation, when we played Indians and cowboys, all of us little Skins fought on the same side against the cowboys in our minds. We never lost.

3.

Indians never lost their West, so how come I walk into the supermarket and find a dozen cowboy books telling me *How The West Was Won?* Curious, I travel to the world's largest shopping mall, find the Lost and Found Department. "Excuse me," I say. "I seem to have lost the West. Has anybody turned it in?" The clerk tells me I can find it in the Sears Home Entertainment Department, blasting away on fifty televisions.

4.

On Saturday morning television, the cowboy has fifty bullets in his six-shooter; he never needs to reload. It's just one more miracle for this country's heroes.

5.

My heroes have never been cowboys; my heroes carry guns in their minds.

6.

Win their hearts and minds and we win the war. Can you hear that song echo across history? If you give the Indian a cup of coffee with six cubes of sugar, he'll be your servant. If you give the Indian a cigarette and a book of matches, he'll be your friend. If you give the Indian a can of commodities, he'll be your lover. He'll hold you tight in his arms, cowboy, and two-step you outside.

7.

Outside it's cold and a confused snow falls in May. I'm watching some western on TBS, colorized, but the story remains the same. Three cowboys string telegraph wire across the plains until they are confronted by the entire Sioux nation. The cowboys, 19th century geniuses, talk the Indians into touching the wire, holding it in their hands and mouths. After a dozen or so have hold of the wire, the cowboys crank the portable generator and electrocute some of the Indians with a European flame and chase the rest of them away, bareback and burned. All these years later, the message tapped across my skin remains the same.

8.

It's the same old story whispered on the television in every HUD house on the reservation. It's 500 years of that same screaming song, translated from the American.

9.

Lester FallsApart found the American dream in a game of Russian Roulette: one bullet and five empty chambers. "It's Manifest Destiny," Lester said just before he pulled the trigger five times quick. "I missed," Lester said just before he reloaded the pistol: one empty chamber and five bullets. "Maybe we should call this Reservation Roulette," Lester said just before he pulled the trigger once at his temple and five more times as he pointed the pistol toward the sky.

10.

Looking up into the night sky, I asked my brother what he thought God looked like and he said "God probably looks like John Wayne."

11.

We've all killed John Wayne more than once. When we burned the ant pile in our backyard, my brother and I imagined those ants were some cavalry or another. When Brian, that insane Indian boy from across the street, suffocated neighborhood dogs and stuffed their bodies into the reservation high school basement, he must have imagined those dogs were cowboys, come back to break another treaty.

12.

Every frame of the black and white western is a treaty; every scene in this elaborate serial is a promise. But what about the reservation home movies? What about the reservation heroes? I remember this: Down near Bull's Pasture, Eugene stood on the pavement with a gallon of tequila under his arm. I watched in the rearview mirror as he raised his arm to wave goodbye and dropped the bottle, glass and dreams of the weekend shattered. After all these years, that moment is still the saddest of my whole life.

13.

Your whole life can be changed by the smallest pain.

14.

Pain is never added to pain. It multiplies. Arthur, here we are again, you and I, fancydancing through the geometric progression of our dreams. Twenty years ago, we never believed we'd lose. Twenty years ago, television was our way of finding heroes and spirit animals. Twenty years ago, we never knew we'd spend the rest of our lives in the reservation of our minds, never knew we'd stand outside the gates of the Spokane Indian Reservation without a key to let ourselves back inside. From a distance, that familiar song. Is it country and western? Is it the sound of hearts breaking? Every song remains the same here in America, this country of the Big Sky and Manifest Destiny, this country of John Wayne and broken treaties. Arthur, I have no words which can save our lives, no words approaching forgiveness, no words flashed across the screen at the reservation drive-in, no words promising either of us top billing. Extras, Arthur, we're all extras.

All I Wanted to Do Was Dance

*Alive. This music rocks
me. I drive the interstate,
watch faces come and go on either
side. I am free to be sung to;
I am free to sing. This woman
can cross any line.*
—JOY HARJO

for Diane

Song

Brown-skinned women
I dreamed of you
long before
any of you decided
to dream about me.
I slept on the top bunk
of my U.S. Army Surplus bed

and pretended one of you was asleep on the bottom bunk
beneath me. Too young to fully understand what that physical
presence would've meant, I still knew it was what I needed. But
like anything believed too hard, those dreams always failed me. I
remember all your names, Indian girls I loved, Dawn, Loretta,
Michelle, Jana, Go-Go, LuLu, all of you Spokane Indian princesses
who never asked me to slow dance

to the music
that always found its way
into the Tribal School
and it wasn't only drums
we heard, you know?
The reservation has a symphony
complicated as any
and we all practiced
the fingering
on the piano, on the pine trees
on the secondhand trumpets

but I was always outside the chords, just a little too short for the
melody, and too skinny for the tempo. Oh, I loved it all from a
distance, from inches and miles away, from a generation removed
it seemed. And I loved you all, crazy and brave, in your young
Indian arrogance

and I love you still
when I see any of you
all these years later
often broken
and defeated by this reservation
by alcohol
and your own failed dreams.
I love you
still

when I see you in the bars, your faces scarred and scared. Sometimes, I think I love you because your failures validate mine and because my successes move me beyond the same boundaries that stop you. I can be as selfish as any white or Indian man. Sometimes, I think I love you because you all still slow dance with the next Indian man who might save you. I can hear your bar voice crack into questions: *What tribe are you? Are you married? How long have you been sober/drunk?* Sometimes, I think I love you

> because it's always easiest
> to love the unloved
> to dream
> about the dreamless
> to watch an Indian woman
> just this side
> of beautiful
> slow dance
> to a sad song
> and never have to worry
> about making her any promises

because this distance I've created is perfect. I can never be hurt. Don't you see? I am afraid; I am not afraid. Don't you understand? I know some of you will die in car wrecks. I know some of you will die of cirrhosis. I know some of you will die of a broken heart. But more than that, I know some of you will live, will learn how to breathe this twentieth century oxygen

> and learn how
> to dance a new dance
> with the rhythm
> only Indians possess
> with the rhythm
> innate
> practiced
> beautiful

and I can hope you'll find your new warriors. Believe me, the Indian men are rising from the alleys and doorways, rising from self-hatred and self-pity, rising up on horses of their own making. Believe me, the warriors are coming back

to take their place beside you
rising
beyond the "just surviving"
singing
those new songs
that sound
exactly
like the old ones.

All I Wanted To Do Was Dance

I haven't danced
in years
Indian or white
but when you asked
I didn't hesitate
and moved
onto the floor with you

feeling hopeful and hopeless. How can I say this and mean it?
How can I say this and make it seem real? I have never danced
with an Indian woman. No, that's not exactly true. I have owl
danced with my mother and sisters. You know the owl dance. The
woman asks the man to dance and if he says no, he has to pay
the woman what she wants and also stand in front of the entire
crowd at the dance and explain why he refused. Let's reverse the
tradition for a moment, enough time for me

to ask you to dance
and if you refuse
you'll have to tell me
why
and you'll pay me
five dollars
enough for gas money
back
to my previous life
back

to that moment when I read my love poem for the white woman
while you sat with another Indian woman, all three of you beauti-
ful, listening. Believe me, I remember you in your red shirt. Maybe
you don't even own a red shirt; maybe you've never worn a red
shirt. But in my memory all I can see was that red shirt, your dark
eyes and skin. Your hair was black, long, perfect, and suddenly I
wanted braids. I wanted to tell you that I knew enough of my lan-
guage to say *I love you*

if it ever came to that moment
if you ever asked me
to cross that river
between us
not across some bridge
real or metaphor
but on the backs of salmon
all of us
terrified and amazed.

Running From The Mafia

I dreamed the Mafia
was chasing us across the Great Plains.
On horseback, we escaped
because the Mafia drove Cadillacs
that kept getting stuck in the mud.

I don't know what this means, don't
even know any Italians
personally, and am ashamed to admit
that I've never stayed awake
during any of the *Godfather* movies

always falling asleep
just before the big scene
everybody talks about for years.
I never even dreamed about the Mafia
while sleeping through a movie about the Mafia

so don't ask me to explain my dreams
which are so often what others call
nightmares. I don't know what it means
to have the Mafia chase us, don't know
what it means to be on horseback

in the 20th century, don't know what
it means to escape again, time
after time, sometimes in a miracle
that only dreams or movies about the Mafia
would ever allow to happen, don't

know why we suddenly arrived
in the nomadic camp of an Indian tribe
without a name. We couldn't speak
their language and they couldn't speak ours
so we were left with only sign language

to explain who the Mafia were
and why they were chasing us, how
life is dangerous and unpredictable
especially in dreams. We joined the tribe
and traveled with them, escaping

the Mafia daily. I don't know how
the dream ended. I woke up

before the final credits rolled
but was alone when I opened my eyes
exhausted and thirsty, reached

for the glass of water
always beside my bed
and drank until full, asked myself
why I think of you now
so often, and how you've entered

my dreams so quickly, but all I have to give you
are a few words in the dark. Maybe
I say *escape*. Maybe I say *horses*.
Maybe I say *Cadillac*. Maybe I whisper
Mafia exactly like I whisper your name.

Billy Jack

Indian woman, Indian man
sit in a Spokane restaurant
and endure those stares again
of the curious or racist: How
do you tell the difference?

But it's you, it's me, sitting
in that Spokane downtown
restaurant when the waiter spills
water into my lap. I rise up
hungry, angry, lonely, tired

as I've had to rise so many times
over the years. First, to survive
my birth and every day since,
to survive other attempts on my life
but I don't say a word this time

to the waiter, who is more clumsy
than racist, who rushes and mumbles
a quick apology. I look to you
because you understand and know
why I was so quick to rage, remember

why my hand closes easily to fist.
We have been in other places
like this, separately and together.
We have sat down in restaurants
where the talk at the next table

turned to redneck discussions
of fishing rights and reservation
border disputes. We have been in
so many places like this, in love,
sweetheart, when you took my hand

brown on brown, and asked
"Where's Billy Jack when you need him?"
Oh, Billy Jack, half-breed hero
of those '70s movies who saved all
the hippies and Indians

from ranchers, farmers, policemen
I remember you. Oh, Billy Jack
I remember how you kicked and punched
all those who kicked and punched
first. Violence against violence.

Oh, Billy Jack, I remember that scene
in the ice cream store when Bernard
terrorizes the reservation kids, pours
flour over the head of an Indian girl
to make her white. I remember watching you

pull up in your jeep across the street/invisible/to no one/except
Bernard/who continued/to torture the Indian kids./How/you
looked around the store/grew/angry/sighed and tried to maintain
control./ *Bernard,* you said/*I want you to know I try./When Jeane
and the kids at the school/tell me that I'm supposed to control/my
violent temper/and be passive and non-violent/like they are/I try/I
really try./But when I see this girl of such a beautiful spirit/so
degraded/and I see this boy that I love/sprawled out by this big
ape here/and this little girl/who is so special to us/that we
call her God's/little gift of sunshine/and I think of the number
of years she's going to have to carry in her memory the savagery/
of this idiotic moment of yours/I just go berserk!/*

Oh, Billy Jack, I cheered then
just like all the other Indians
who ever saw your movies. I think
all Indians saw your movies, wanted you
to be real, wanted you to rise

and save the Indians from their sins.
But all these years later, we need more.
Indian woman, Indian man sit
in a Spokane restaurant, touch hand
to hand, palms open, palms together

in a shared prayer. You and I know, sweetheart,
that we have been in a place
like this, separately and together,
you and me and Billy Jack,
a place called the United States of America.

Now we have been here long enough, and soon
we will stand up, pay our bill, walk out
the door and leave it all behind us. It's time
and I've got news for everyone else
so they won't be surprised when they get to Heaven:

God has dark skin.

First Indian on the Moon

Can I tell you now
that I've dreamed of your hair
in a good way?

I've dreamed your hair
could save us all.

Its length is a rope
for climbing ivory walls.
Its strength is a knot
for holding Skins together.
Its smell is the smoke
from the powwow campfire.
Its shine is the moonlight
and its shine makes you

the first Indian on the moon.
The first Indian on the moon
is a woman.
The first Indian on the moon
is you
and if my dream is long
as your hair
and if my dream is strong
as your hair

then maybe you can let all your hair down
find me somewhere alone on earth
and maybe I can reach up and take hold.
Maybe you can let all your hair down
and maybe I can reach up and take hold.
Maybe you can let all your hair down
and maybe I can reach up and take hold

and although the whites say
you can't hear anything in space
I say we'll hear each other breathe
I say we'll hear each other move
I say we'll hear each other whisper
I love you
and I will say it in my own language
I'll say it in the little piece
of my own language that I know
and I'll say it like it's the last thing I'll ever say:

quye han-xm=enc, quye han-xm=enc, quye han-xm=enc.